Harvest of Souls
The Jesuit Missions
and Colonialism in North America, 1632–1650

In *Harvest of Souls* Carole Blackburn uses the *Jesuit Relations* to shed light on the dialogue between Jesuit missionaries and the Native peoples of northeastern North America, providing a historical anthropology of two cultures attempting to understand, contend with, and accommodate each other in the new world.

In 1632 Jesuit missionary Paul Le Jeune, newly arrived at the fort of Quebec, wrote the first of the *Relations* to his superior in Paris, initiating a series of mission reports that came to be known as the *Jesuit Relations*. Blackburn presents a contemporary interpretation of the 1632–1650 *Relations*, arguing that they are colonizing texts in which the Jesuits use language, imagery, and forms of knowledge to legitimize relations of inequality with the Huron and Montagnais.

By combining textual analysis with an ethnographic study of the Jesuits, Blackburn is able to reveal the gap between the domineering language of the *Relations* and the limited authority that the Jesuits were able to exercise over Native people, who actively challenged much of what the Jesuits tried to do and say. She highlights the struggle between the Jesuits and Natives over the meaning of Christianity. The Jesuits attempted to convey their Christian message through Native languages and cultural idioms. Blackburn shows that this resulted in the displacement of much of the content of the message and demonstrates that the Native people's acts of resistance took up and transformed aspects of the Jesuits' teachings in ways that subverted their authority.

Harvest of Souls is essential for all those interested in new approaches to historical and contemporary relations between Europeans and Native peoples in North America.

CAROLE BLACKBURN is a doctoral student in anthropology at Stanford University.

McGILL-QUEEN'S NATIVE AND NORTHERN SERIES
BRUCE G. TRIGGER, EDITOR

1 When the Whalers Were
Up North
Inuit Memories from the
Eastern Arctic
Dorothy Harley Eber

2 The Challenge of Arctic
Shipping
Science, Environmental
Assessment, and Human Values
David L. VanderZwaag and
Cynthia Lamson, Editors

3 Lost Harvests
Prairie Indian Reserve Farmers
and Government Policy
Sarah Carter

4 Native Liberty, Crown
Sovereignty
The Existing Aboriginal Right
of Self-Government in Canada
Bruce Clark

5 Unravelling the Franklin
Mystery
Inuit Testimony
David C. Woodman

6 Otter Skins, Boston Ships, and
China Goods
The Maritime Fur Trade of the
Northwest Coast,
1785–1841
James R. Gibson

7 From Wooden Ploughs to
Welfare
The Story of the Western
Reserves
Helen Buckley

8 In Business for Ourselves
Northern Entrepreneurs
Wanda A. Wuttunee

9 For an Amerindian Autohistory
An Essay on the Foundations
of a Social Ethic
Georges E. Sioui

10 Strangers Among Us
David Woodman

11 When the North Was Red
Aboriginal Education in Soviet
Siberia
Dennis A. Bartels and
Alice L. Bartels

12 From Talking Chiefs to a
Native Corporate Elite
The Birth of Class and
Nationalism among Canadian
Inuit
Marybelle Mitchell

13 Cold Comfort
My Love Affair with the
Arctic
Graham W. Rowley

14 The True Spirit and Original
Intent of Treaty 7
Treaty 7 Elders and Tribal
Council with Walter
Hildebrandt, Dorothy First
Rider, and Sarah Carter

15 This Distant and Unsurveyed
Country
A Woman's Winter at Baffin
Island, 1857–1858
W. Gillies Ross

16 Images of Justice
   Dorothy Harley Eber

17 Capturing Women
   The Manipulation of Cultural
   Imagery in Canada's
   Prairie West
   Sarah A. Carter

18 Social and Environmental
   Impacts of the James Bay
   Hydroelectric Project
   Edited by
   James F. Hornig

19 Saqiyuq
   Stories from the Lives of
   Three Inuit Women
   *Nancy Wachowich in
   collaboration with Apphia
   Agalakti Awa, Rhoda Kaukjak
   Katsak, and Sandra Pikujak
   Katsak*

20 Justice in Paradise
   Bruce Clark

21 Aboriginal Rights and
   Self-Government
   The Canadian and Mexican
   Experience in North American
   Perspective
   *Edited by Curtis Cook and
   Juan D. Lindau*

22 Harvest of Souls
   The Jesuit Missions
   and Colonialism in North
   America, 1632–1650
   Carole Blackburn

Harvest of Souls

The Jesuit Missions and Colonialism in North America, *1632–1650*

Carole Blackburn

for Renato,
from Carole

McGill-Queen's University Press

Montreal & Kingston · London · Ithaca

© McGill-Queen's University Press 2000
ISBN 0-7735-2047-3

Legal deposit second quarter 2000
Bibliothèque nationale du Québec

Printed in Canada on acid-free paper

This book has been published with the help of a grant
from the Humanities and Social Sciences Federation of
Canada, using funds provided by the Social Sciences
and Humanities Research Council of Canada.

McGill-Queen's University Press acknowledges the
financial support of the Government of Canada
through the Book Publishing Industry Development
Program (BPIDP) for its activities. We also
acknowledge the support of the Canada Council for
the Arts for our publishing program.

Canadian Cataloguing in Publication Data

Blackburn, Carole, 1963–
    Harvest of souls : the Jesuit missions and colonialism
    in North America, 1632–1650
    (McGill-Queen's native and northern series)
    Includes bibliographical references and index.
    ISBN 0-7735-2047-3
    1. Jesuits – Missions – Canada – History – 17th
    century. 2. Indians of North America – Canada –
    Missions – History – 17th century. I. Title.
    FC315.B63 2000   266'.271   C99-901345-9
    F1030.7.B63 2000

Typeset in Sabon 10.5/13
by Caractéra inc., Quebec City

Contents

Acknowledgments   ix

Illustrations   xi

1   Introduction   3

2   Jesuit Beginnings in New France   21

3   The Wilderness   42

4   Law and Order   70

5   Conversion and Conquest   105

Conclusion   129

Notes   141

References   157

Index   169

Acknowledgments

This book would not have been possible without the support and encouragement of a number of people. I am indebted to Bruce Trigger for first encouraging me to develop this manuscript out of my master's thesis, as well as for his insightful comments on the text and terminology. This book is a considerably reworked and expanded version of that thesis, and I have learned as much during the process of expanding it as I did during its first writing. I would like to thank Toby Morantz again for her guidance and generosity during the years she was my thesis director at McGill University. I also thank Ken Little, Colin Scott, and Carmen Lambert for their contributions to the original thesis, as well as my student friends and colleagues during my years in Montreal. Jane Collier, Nicholas De Genova, and Blair Rutherford provided valuable suggestions on the revised and expanded text as well as encouragement. I am also grateful to the three anonymous reviewers whose thoughtful comments and criticisms helped me improve the manuscript. Miyako Inoue also gave valuable comments on a shorter version of some of the arguments presented here, when I developed them in the context of her graduate seminar on language and political economy at Stanford. For insights into life and publishing, I am indebted to Dara Culhane. Any errors and deficiencies in the present work are of course mine alone.

At McGill-Queen's University Press, Aurèle Parisien offered encouragement and helpful comments on the book from the very beginning. I would also like to thank Joan McGilvray for guiding the manuscript through production and Carlotta Lemieux for her fine editorial skills. I am grateful as well for the help of the staff at the National Library and National Archives of Canada.

I also thank my parents for supporting my academic endeavours over the years. Finally, I thank Ninan, to whom this book is dedicated, for his support, enthusiasm and patience throughout.

LE R P PAVL le IEVNE enflamé d'vn st. zele pour la conuersion des Infideles, Sauuages de la Nouuelle France, fut le premier qui
les suiuit dans les bois les frequenta recomut leur humeur, et en aprit leur langue la reduisit en preceptes; il n'est pas croyable combien il souffrit de
froid, de chaud, de faim en ses courses dans les rigueurs de plusieurs Ryuers, et estoit parmy ces barbares qui le plus souuent estoient sur le point de l'asom-
mer, et dont il a euité miraculeusement la fureur, ce sont les preuues de son ardeur pour l'augmentation de nostre Religion pour la gloire de Dieu; il
passa dix-sept ans dans le Canada, d'ou apres auoir faict Nombre de conuersions de ces Infidelles, il fut rapelé en l'Ancienne France son pays
natal pour les affaires de cette Mission, et en estre le Procureur, pour l'interest de laquelle il a agi auec soing continuel, iusqu'à ce qu'il rendit
sa bien-heureuse Ame entre les mains de son Sauueur chargé de Merittes et consommé dans les trauaux spirituels le 7e. d'Aoust 1664. agé de 72 ans

R. Lochon Sculbat et excudebat.   Cum priuilegio Regis 1665.

Paul Le Jeune, 1591–1664 (courtesy of National Archives of Canada [NA],
C-21404)

Western half of the *Novae Franciae Accurata Delineatio*, 1657.
This wonderfully illustrated map is thought to have been drawn by Father
Bressani. Original in the National Library, Paris (courtesy NA, NMC-6338)

Le Canada, ou Nouvelle-France, published by N. Sanson d'Abbeville in 1656 (courtesy NA, NMC-21100)

Carte géographique de la Nouvelle France by Samuel de Champlain. This map was published in Champlain's *Voyages* in 1613. The inset depicts a Montagnais man, woman, and child on the left and two figures identified as Abenaki (Almouchiquois) on the right. Original in the National Library of Canada (courtesy National Library of Canada, NMC-6327)

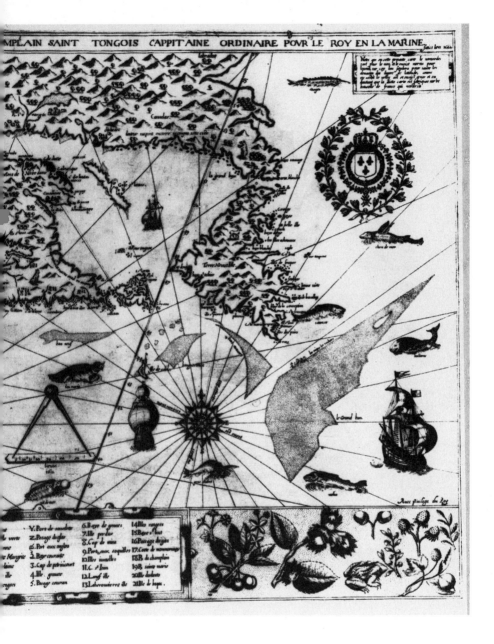

An Aboriginal family praying. Detail from Bressani's *Novae Franciae Accurata Delineatio*, 1657. Original in National Library, Paris (courtesy NA, C-71502)

Harvest of Souls

Introduction

Every image of the past that is not recognized by the present as one
of its own concerns threatens to disappear irretrievably.

Walter Benjamin, *Illuminations*

In 1640 the Jesuit missionary Paul Le Jeune described the outcome
of a meeting of newly converted Christians residing in the small
community of Sillery, near the French fort of Quebec. These Christians, who were among the most zealous of those living at Sillery,
had met during the winter "in order to confer together upon the
means of keeping themselves in the faith" (Thwaites 1896–1901,
20:143–5; hereafter cited by volume and page number). According
to Le Jeune, one of these Christians, "in making an address, said
that he thought more highly of prayers – it is thus that they speak
– than of life, and that he would rather die than give them up;
another said that he wished he might be punished and chastised in
case he forfeited the word he had given to God; a third exclaimed
that he who should fall into any error must be put into prison, and
made to fast four days without eating or drinking" (20:143–5).
This statement appears in the *Relation* of 1640–41, almost ten
years after Le Jeune first arrived at Quebec as the superior of the
Jesuits' mission in New France and wrote the first of his *Relations*
to his superior in Paris.[1] As I shall show throughout this book, the
devotion, obedience, and willingness to submit to punishment
expressed by the Aboriginal men who were party to this discussion
could not be more in keeping with the Jesuits' hopes for the
progress of the Roman Catholic faith in the New World. At the same
time, these sentiments could not be more in contrast with the
responses – also described in the *Relations* – of many other Aboriginal people, who either rejected Christianity entirely or adopted it
as part of their larger spiritual repertoire in a way that suggests
that they understood neither the absolutist, universalist aspect of

the Christian message nor the necessity of complete obedience and submission.

The issues for those who read the Jesuits' voluminous *Relations* and encounter statements such as Le Jeune's are multiple and complex. They are also the subject of this book. Readers, scholars, and critics have commented on the content of the *Relations* from the time Le Jeune and others first put their pens to paper; some disparaged them as propaganda, while others found inspiration in them for pious labours at home and abroad. The *Relations* were written between 1611 and 1791 and were published until 1673.[2] They were later republished, with the addition of a variety of associated documents, under the editorship of Rueben Gold Thwaites, at the end of the nineteenth century. This republication occurred at a time of renewed interest in the history of New France and the colonial Northeast generally, and it made the *Relations* widely available to historians in an accessible format, placing the original French and Latin alongside an English translation. Historians and, more recently, ethnohistorians of seventeenth- and eighteenth-century northeastern North America continue to use the *Relations* as primary source material.[3] Putting them to this kind of use, however, requires some attention to the question of their reliability as sources. Le Jeunes's description of the zeal of new Christians, for example, paints a provocative picture of the effects of the Jesuits' mission but begs the question of what parts of the *Relations* can be used in historical and ethnographic reconstruction, and what parts primarily reflect the Jesuits' particular world view and missionary agenda.

The question of distortion is especially important in the case of the Jesuits' often lengthy descriptions of the customs of the Aboriginal people among whom they made their mission. This question is also most closely related to the focus of this book although, as I shall soon show, my analysis is concerned with the entirety of the Jesuits' descriptions of Aboriginal people, including what is now easily recognized as biased. While the authenticity of the Jesuits' descriptions of conversion was an issue even when the *Relations* were first published, detailed attention to their descriptions of Native people has been more important for contemporary scholars, notably, ethnohistorians and anthropologists. The Jesuits did not inhabit a world in which an idea of culture as an integrated set of meanings, symbols, or behavioural norms was the fundamental repository for observed differences; in this sense they were unlike the anthropologists and ethnohistorians who would read their texts three centuries later. However, they were the heirs of a Renaissance humanism that had engendered considerable interest in the study and collection of information on the "piece of work" that was humankind.[4] This included the increasingly systematic collection and description of differences in the customs, traits, and manners of people both in Europe and abroad. The *Relations* thus combine descriptions of the allegedly savage and superstitious practices of Native people with careful accounts of their economies, material culture, ritual practices, and political structures.

For many ethnohistorians, these semi-ethnographic portions of the text are a valuable record of the lifeways of Aboriginal people in the St Lawrence region in the seventeenth century and are fairly easily distinguished from the interpretive excesses that stem from the Jesuits' assumptions about savagery and their own superiority. Elisabeth Tooker has used the *Relations*, in combination with the writings of Samuel de Champlain and the Recollet missionary Gabriel Sagard, as a primary source for an ethnography of the Huron for the period between 1615 and 1649. Tooker recommends that while the *Relations* "should not be read uncritically, the cautions are few" ([1964] 1991, 7). She suggests that the Jesuits' biases should now be obvious and therefore easily dismissed, and that their descriptions of Aboriginal cultures should be assessed for accuracy by comparing them with the existing ethnographic record (ibid.).

Bruce Trigger has used the *Relations* in an analysis of the history of the Huron people, who were the focus of Jesuit missionary activity in New France between 1635 and 1650. He argues that the Jesuits' texts may be used as "reliable, though partial, sources of information about this period" (1987, 472). Conrad Heidenreich (1971, 311), who refers to the *Jesuit Relations* as source material in his reconstruction of the historical geography of Huronia, argues that they provide valuable information on some, although not all, aspects of Huron life. Kenneth Morrison (1986, 3) advocates one of the more literal approaches, suggesting that the *Relations* "present accurate ethnological descriptions of Montagnais life," both in records of what the Montagnais said and in descriptions of how they acted. While the *Relations* do contain accurate descriptions of some of the lifeways of the Aboriginal people who lived in the St Lawrence valley, recent debates in anthropology suggest that even descriptions that are made with careful attention to accuracy and attempt to produce a picture of a culture in its entirety are incomplete. My own analysis will emphasize the partial nature of the Jesuits' descriptions over their fullness and literal accuracy.

Le Jeune's description of the zeal of the new Christians at Sillery speaks primarily to the transformation wrought by the Jesuits on indigenous ways of life. It also raises the question of whether the degree of devotion and willing submission expressed by these and other converts is an accurate depiction of their intentions and their understanding of Christianity, or whether it is an exaggeration inspired by the Jesuits' desire to present their endeavours in the New World in the best possible light. Both supporters and detractors of the Jesuit order and its mission policies read the published *Relations*. This has long been a backdrop to interpretations of the Jesuits' depiction of their work as missionaries and of the piety of those Native people who apparently did embrace Christianity. A consideration of Le Jeune's description involves not only an assessment of the reliability of the Jesuits' texts but also some measure of speculation concerning the likelihood that Native people actually understood the message the Jesuits were trying to convey. Some scholars have argued that the accounts of Native conversions in the *Relations* are neither exaggerations inspired by propagandist necessity nor culturally implausible (Morrison 1990, 433; Campeau 1987, 356–9). Lucien Campeau, for example, defends the integrity of the conversions described in the *Relations* from the Huron mission on the basis of the universal human relevance of Christianity, as well as the Hurons' receptive religious sensibilities (1987, 356–9). Similarly Morrison, who addresses the question of the conversions brought about by the Jesuits among small numbers of Montagnais, argues that "the Jesuits did not exaggerate" when "reporting what they saw as the workings of grace" (1990, 433).

Yet assessments of the piety of Christian converts are often based on a literal reading of speeches attributed to Aboriginal people in the *Relations*. Although the Jesuits defended the accuracy of these transcriptions, their defence frequently included the regret that they could not convey the eloquence of the speaker adequately in French translation (e.g., 19:41; 20:225; 25;257). The likelihood of misunderstandings being incorporated in translations that were based on varying degrees of competence in Native languages, as well as the possibility of errors occurring in the act of transcription, caution against a strictly literal understanding of these speeches. In addition, when one considers the more "general tendency of European authors of the time to embellish and to fabricate whole addresses" (Trigger 1987, 17), the literal detail with which the priests claimed to represent Native speakers becomes even more questionable.[5]

Material the Jesuits wrote exclusively for use within the mission was also less orthodox and less recognizably Christian than the accounts of either the Jesuits' teaching or the Aboriginal people's reception of this teaching as depicted in the *Relations* (Steckley 1992, 480). In the Huron *Relation* of 1636, for example, the Jesuit Jean de Brébeuf referred to the difficulty of translating the meaning of the Trinity into the Huron language and requested approval to render it as "In the name of our Father, and of his Son, and of their holy Ghost" (10:119–21). However, later in that century, the Jesuits prepared religious instruction in the Huron language that represented the three persons of the Trinity more liberally: as *sa,oen*, which is translated as "he has them [indefinite] as children," *honaen*, meaning "they [masculine or feminine] have him as a child," and *hoki daat hoatato,eti*, meaning "he is a very [straight] spirit" (ibid.).[6] It is doubtful that this accommodation would have been either acceptable to the Jesuits' supporters or defensible if subjected to the scrutiny of their critics.

Certainly, the Jesuits were relatively successful as missionaries (Axtell 1985, 276–9), and their descriptions of their successes are not solely exaggerations. However, their need to create a favourable impression in the minds of potential financial supporters, as well as their need to gain points against their critics, cannot be overlooked in any consideration of the ideals of Christian piety and devotion represented in the *Relations*. On more than one occasion, the Jesuits referred to the *Relations* and their accounts of the good behaviour of Christians as a form of tribute which their audience expected them to provide (8:215, 14:123, 31:139). Whether intentionally or not, the Jesuits used their *Relations* to advance points of doctrine and theology, and their representations of newly converted Christians were useful devices for illustrating the possibility of natural grace and for arguing that all human beings were capable of salvation (Berkhofer 1979, 74). It is largely in relation to this emphasis in the Jesuits' texts that several authors have remarked on the importance of the Jesuits' *Relations* in providing the raw material for the "noble savage" of Rousseau and others during the eighteenth century (ibid.; Honour 1975, 120–1; Healy 1958, 144; Symcox 1972, 227).[7] Insofar as the Jesuits did occasionally evoke images of noble savagery, this aspect of their writing should be as subject to critique as any other, regardless of its more appealing quality.[8] The criteria for accuracy in colonial accounts cannot simply be whether or not the accounts are sympathetic or unsympathetic to the people they represent.

There are more questions to ask, however, of Le Jeune's depiction of the Sillery Christians, and of the *Relations* in general, than those that are geared only toward distinguishing between true and false representations. If Le Jeune's description is exaggerated, which I suggest it is, this statement and others that share the same emphasis or speak even more directly to the Jesuits' expectations that Aboriginal people submit to them, as well as to God, are nevertheless valuable indices of the motivations, expectations, and assumptions which the Jesuits brought to their encounter with Aboriginal people in the Northeast. Rather than simply separating material that is empirically sound from the more obviously biased portion of the *Relations*, I intend to examine the intent, effect, and meaning of the texts in their entirety. Although this includes, initially, situating the Jesuits' statements in relation to such factors as their need to impress critics, this kind of contextualizing is only part of my critical purpose and interpretive method.

While Le Jeune took care to describe, for example, the characteristics of the Montagnais' hunting practices and methods of food preparation, he also wrote that the people were "only fed like dogs; for their most splendid feastings are, so to speak, only the bones and the leavings of the tables of Europe!" (6:251). In these and other accounts of savage habits, he and subsequent authors of the *Relations* characterized non-Christian Native people as raw, untamed subjects, inferior to Europeans, and implicitly in need of the Jesuits' particular agenda of tutelage and transformation. In my engagement with the entirety of the Jesuits' accounts, I approach the *Relations* as a valuable site for an exploration of the pursuit and effects of power, and its justification, as well as for looking at the power of language to naturalize – through rhetorical forms, strategies, idioms, and categories of expression – the "structures of domination" (Dirks 1992b, 175).

I am guided in this approach by the insights and methods of colonial discourse studies and historical anthropology. It is a principle of colonial discourse studies that colonialism relied on the production and manipulation of forms of knowledge as much as it involved particular configurations of economic and military power (Young 1995, 163; Said 1993, 9). Colonial documents, whether the product of missionaries, such as the Jesuits, or of explorers, officials, or administrators, were instrumental in producing a body of knowledge about the colonized and colonizers that both came from and shaped the ideologies informing colonialism. This knowledge was linked to the technology of colonial rule. Indeed, administrators often systematically acquired this knowledge in order to make rule more effective (Cohn 1985, 283; Prakash 1992, 357). In this respect, texts were not just the byproducts of a political process; nor are their frequently pejorative depictions of the colonized merely evidence of the ethnocentrism of an earlier, less tolerant age. They were, rather, a more integral component of the politics of colonialism, because they expressed the themes, ideas, and ideologies that served domination and justified the colonial endeavour. They also defined an arena of knowledge about the colonized and the colonial endeavour generally, which limited what could be recognized as the truth.

In the *Jesuit Relations* the representations of Aboriginal peoples quickly took the form of authoritative descriptions, made credible by the priests' claims that they described only what they had seen with their own eyes or had personally experienced (6:263; 7:35; 10:171; 14:59–63).[9] While the Jesuits did not evoke culture and did not look for the form and function of organically defined, unique social units, in the manner of latter-day ethnographers, they did search for and expect to find customs, traits, and manners that were permanent and by which the people they wrote about could be identified. In setting out the nature of their subjects, the Jesuits created a category of savagery that relied on a generalizing logic of rigidity and predictability. Le Jeune's description of the first people he saw when he arrived in North America, for example, began with the specifics of their individual painted faces but was soon cast in general terms as he dealt with modes of dress in winter and summer, "their" intelligence, and "their" physique (5:21–5). This logic is a mainstay of colonial discourses that claim to represent the subjects of colonialism, and it effectively homogenizes the natives into a knowable other, uncomplicated by historical change, by contradiction, or by the accident of individual circumstances.

Generally, once traits are determined as characteristic they become self-fulfilling and self-perpetuating, and may be represented without question (Bhabba 1994, 66).

Colonial discourse studies thus look at the discursive dimension of colonialism as a critical arena for studying how relations of domination are articulated as well as how the forms of knowledge that enabled and sustained colonial rule were produced. This is not, generally, an apolitical exercise in the reading of texts that no longer have any relevance or are no longer representative of larger systems of meaning and the political structures related to them. The best work in colonial discourse studies represents a politically engaged strategy of reading that seeks to dismantle and decentre what colonial representations depicted as self-evident; in the process, these studies challenge the received understanding of conventional historiography, in which civilization (and/or progress) is depicted as advancing across and enlightening the darker places of the globe. The point is to uncover and denaturalize the categories that were used to marginalize and disenfranchise colonized peoples, as well as those categories that were used to legitimate the power of the dominant over the dominated. This includes the seemingly obvious or natural differences between savagery and civilization, tradition and modernity, East and West, as well as what appeared from these differentiations to be both inevitable, like progress, and necessary, like salvation.

For many scholars, the point of identifying the themes, ideas, and values that served domination in the past is to speak to the legacy of this domination in the present and to the current configurations of power, along with the knowledge that legitimates them. Although the colonial empires that are recalled in contemporary forms of imperialist nostalgia are now dissolved, colonialism continues, and it is not exclusively a Western phenomenon.[10] European colonialism was but a form of imperialism, and the latter "lingers where it has always been, in a kind of general cultural sphere as well as in specific political, ideological, economic and social practices" (Said 1993, 12). Certainly, economic, cultural, and political imperialism continues without colonies. We can better understand the stark inequalities of our globalized world if we look at them in historical perspective, that is, in relation to the political, economic, and social structures created through the centuries of Western colonial expansion and imperialism (Williams and Chrisman 1994, 4).

Written more than three centuries ago, the *Jesuit Relations* are a rich and important partial archive of one portion of the multifaceted relationship between Native peoples and Europeans on this continent. My purpose is to uncover the logic that underlies the Jesuits' accounts of their activities and their perceptions of Aboriginal peoples, thereby speaking to a past that continues to matter very much in the present, and thus contributing, however partially, to writing the history of this present. This involves identifying the principal themes of the *Relations*, including their many contradictions and ambiguities, and the hierarchical vision that these themes served. I focus on the *Relations* written between 1632, when the Jesuits entered New France with a monopoly on mission activity there, and 1650, when the Huron confederacy and the Jesuits' mission in it collapsed. My intention in pursuing the sedimented meanings that inhabit the Jesuits' texts is not to produce a history of ideas but to situate these meanings in relation to the politics of colonialism and conversion, and to illustrate how they reveal an agenda that required Aboriginal people to be, by and large, subordinated to the Jesuits. It is because of this emphasis on subordination – both to the priests and to the logic of the world view which the priests' wished to impose – that I characterize the *Jesuit Relations* as colonial texts, even though this period in the history of New France was characterized by minimal settlement and the absence of either French rule or French dominance (Comaroff 1997, 182).

My aim is to combine the above purposes with the goals of historical anthropology and, in so doing, to cast the critical lens of ethnography on the Jesuits in a way that not only pursues the various meanings in their *Relations* but also examines the ways in which they struggled with Native people over the creation of meaning in New France. This struggle is spoken to in the Jesuits' texts, but it must also be understood in relation to the contingencies that shaped the Jesuits' mission and their relationship with Aboriginal people. I thus attend to the extradiscursive dimension of this encounter and to the limits of discourse in a way that separates my approach from that of those who focus on the rhetorical or narrative features of the *Relations*; or those who use them, either exclusively or in conjunction with other primary documents, to write histories of European images of New World alterity.[11] In addition, because I focus principally on the common themes and enduring features of the *Relations*, my work is unlike that of scholars who emphasize individual authorship and treat the *Relations* as a gateway to the psychology of specific priests (e.g., Ouellet 1987, 1993; Pioffet 1993).

Indeed, my attention to the extradiscursive dimension of the *Relations* is made in relation to the criticism that the textual focus of colonial discourse studies often appears to be removed from the experience of colonialism, sometimes illuminating more of the fantasmatics of the colonial imagination than the relationship between discourses and the contexts to which they refer (Young 1995, 160; Dirks 1992b, 175). I do not use context here to refer to an independent reality that is apart from either the texts or the processes of colonialism itself; they are all products of each other and cannot be easily separated. The point is that in the case of the *Jesuit Relations*, it is possible, while illuminating the coercive intent that informs the Jesuits' writings, to accord too much authority to the texts and the visions they promulgate. This has the effect of reifying the Jesuits' discourse and allowing it an independent existence apart from the social actors and events that it describes. It also erases the agency of the Aboriginal participants in the encounter and ignores the struggles over meaning and the conceptual slippages which, I suggest, were an integral backdrop to the *Relations* and an inevitable feature of the Jesuits' work as missionaries. While a literal reading of the *Relations* can support a thesis that the Jesuits achieved a radical, rapid, and thorough decline in the status of women in the Montagnais and Huron populations (Anderson 1991), such a reading is not critical of, but is complicit with, the Jesuits' representations of their own power and influence (Dirks 1992a, 14).

The expression of dominance in the *Relations* is, I suggest, not necessarily equivalent to dominance in their actual relationship with Native people. While identifying the signs on which the Jesuits built their authority, it is important to question the extent of that authority. The Jesuits make many comments in the *Relations* that situate indigenous people in a subordinate position to themselves, or more generally to the French. Le Jeune, for example, referred to the Huron boys who joined the Jesuits' fledgling and soon-to-fail school for boys at Quebec as "hostages" (9:283).[12] Ouellet and Beaulieu (1993, 19) point out that this word conveys the sense that "les enfants des alliés ne sont plus des enfants, mais, de gré ou de force, des prises militaires."[13] The rhetorical effect of the militant language used by the Jesuits needs full emphasis; however, as I suggested above, the power actually wielded by the priests requires as much critical study as the desire for power that was revealed in their texts. While Le Jeune's readers may have been impressed by the strength of the word "hostage" and the authority its use implied, at the time when Le Jeune used the word, neither the Jesuits nor any of the other French had the ability to restrain the boys against their will. The situation of the Jesuits and the French before implementation of what is known as the royal regime in 1663 was tenuous, both economically and militarily, and the domination which they may have wished to exert in their relations with Aboriginal people was often impossible.

It is also important to distinguish between the effect of this word in the rhetorical universe of the *Relations* and the practice it referred to in the context of early-seventeenth-century trading relationships in northeastern North America. Le Jeune's term is less forceful and less indicative of the capacity of the Jesuits to exploit or control Native people when one considers that at the time Europeans began trading in the St Lawrence, Aboriginal groups often exchanged people with their trading allies as an expression of goodwill (Heidenreich 1971, 221). Samuel de Champlain had arranged for French boys to live among the Huron and Algonkin in the expectation that they would learn the language and provide future service as interpreters and intermediaries in the fur trade. In doing this, he was confronted with the assumption by the Huron and Algonkin that they would reciprocally send some of their people to live among the French (Biggar [1922–36] 1971, 2:138–42, 186–8, 201–2). It was partly as a consequence of these exchanges that a number of Huron and Algonkin boys were taken to France in the early seventeenth century (Trigger 1971, 89).[14]

Champlain was not always so willing to accommodate indigenous practices; but his willingness to participate in these exchanges and his awareness of the responsibility he bore in meeting the obligations surrounding them, including the proper treatment and return of the boys, helped cement the alliances between himself and the Huron and Algonkin (Biggar [1922–36] 1971, 2:189). The Huron traders who took the Jesuit fathers with them into Huronia would have viewed the priests as guarantees of the good faith and alliance of their French counterparts, just as they would have viewed the young men and boys who had preceded the priests in living among them. In this way, the Jesuits and other French who lived among trading allies during this time were equally, in a sense, hostages. The Jesuits would have understood this, for they were not politically naive and were well aware of their vulnerability during their years in the Huron mission.

Thus, while colonial discourse analysis is based on the position that representations matter and have real effects, it is critical to ask to what extent they matter and to whom (Mani 1992, 394). This questioning forms part of the critique of colonialism itself, as it rejects the totalizing effects of colonial representations in favour of a more nuanced understanding of the relationships between colonizers and colonized. The Jesuits wrote of dominance and dreamed of hegemony, but I suggest that the former was difficult if not initially unrealizable and that the latter was impossible during the first half of the seventeenth century. There was no colonial state in New France between 1632 and 1650, nor was there even colonial rule. The inequalities that did emerge during the first half of the seventeenth century, and that will be important in this analysis, arose less through rule by force than through the loss of game resources, and the debilitating and ultimately catastrophic effects of disease and warfare that were themselves direct or indirect consequences of French involvement in the Northeast. Many Aboriginal people, including the Huron and the Montagnais living in the vicinity of Quebec, became economically tied to the French; this reduced their autonomy and gave the Jesuits and other French a measure of advantage over them.

However, even when a colonial state is firmly in place and a colonized population exists in a subjugated position, it is a mistake to equate the dominance of the rulers with hegemony (Guha 1989, 228). Hegemony is not easily defined but is a useful concept when considering the impact of the Jesuits. It implies a shared realm of meaning between those who hold power and those without it, and enables rule through the force of this meaning, which appears self-evident, rather than through force per se (Comaroff and Comaroff 1991, 23). It also implies the consent of the ruled to be ruled, and the presence of a "political capacity to generate consent through the institutional spaces of civil society" (Dirks 1992a, 7). In this sense it requires continual reproduction with the assistance of things such as schools, and while it is effective because of its apparent seamlessness, people can and do ultimately contest it. The Jesuits' desire "to enter into" the "mind and hearts" (28:65) of Aboriginal people suggests that they were aiming for just this kind of penetration of and control over people's consciousness. However, I suggest that the ability to achieve such control was not a feature of the Jesuits' mission or of the French relationship with Native people generally, during the first half of the seventeenth century.

The authors of colonial texts commonly described the colonized in a way that denied them any agency and placed them within histories that were not of their own making. This is an important feature of the Jesuits' writing, which depicted North America and its inhabitants as a land abandoned, lost to time, and recuperable only through the agency of Europeans. It is also one of the ways in which the Jesuits' texts reveal the themes of colonization, even in its strict absence. Much of the historiography of the Northeast and North America more generally has also privileged Europeans as the principal agents of history, with the result that Aboriginal people have been represented as part of the background against which the movement of European history took place (Jaenen 1974, 291). As I hope will be evident throughout this book, the Aboriginal people who interacted with the Jesuits were not the passive recipients of the priests' assumptions or assertions. In many cases they actively resisted them, and in all cases they subjected the behaviour of the Jesuits (and other Europeans who came among them) to interpretation according to their own views of appropriate human conduct, as well as of the world and the forces that controlled its operation.

Some of these interpretations are partly evident in the *Relations* and will be discussed in the course of this book, particularly in the context of Aboriginal views of the Jesuits' role in creating – as sorcerers – the illnesses to which Native people had so little resistance. Such interpretations were instrumental in contributing to the shape of the encounter and the Jesuits' comprehension and representation of it while the priests and the Aboriginal people they worked among struggled to define the meaning of the events that shaped their mutual engagement. The Jesuits had an advantage in their texts, because in the pages of the *Relations* they could control issues which they could not control in their daily interaction with Aboriginal people. Indeed, the *Relations* were crafted by the Jesuits to enact rhetorical control over debates which Aboriginal peoples

themselves may have found far from over. The *Relations* have of
course come down to us and can be revisited by contemporary
readers. The content of Aboriginal interpretations of Europeans is
less known and, more importantly, these interpretations have not
assumed hegemonic form in dominant discourses. The ability to
interpret and appropriate the behaviour of others is not equivalent
to the ability to establish these interpretations as dominant rhetoric
in the context of emerging political inequalities, or to defend them
as obvious truths in the face of competing interpretations.

Although Aboriginal people argued with and resisted the Jesuits,
I am not suggesting that their interaction was in the form of two
opposing cultures coming into blunt opposition. Rather, I see it as
a process of negotiation and struggle over meaning in which diverse
ideas informed and transformed each other, all in a broader context
of shifting relations of power. It is possible to romanticize resistance
by overemphasizing it; it is also possible to perpetuate a dichotomous image of the colonizers and the colonized – separated by a
gulf of difference and a gulf of power. This image served the idea
of colonialism itself but did not necessarily characterize colonial
relationships (Parry 1987, 28–9). While colonial discourse studies
aim to decentre the West from its self-proclaimed position as the
motor of history and to expose the reified depiction of the colonized
in colonial texts, this approach is most successful as a counterdis-
course when it eliminates the idea of a unitary, unified West. It is
also most successful when it does not replace the artificial homogeneity conferred on subject populations with one that claims to
be more accurate or authentic (cf. Prakash 1992, 376). Although I
have referred to Aboriginal practices and resistance, it is not my
intention to uncover a pure Aboriginal context or voice from the
pages of the *Relations*. That is impossible, given the mediated
nature of much of this voice, and because the Jesuits did not
encounter a single, unified Aboriginal population or unified Aboriginal subjectivity. Native people brought a multiplicity of viewpoints
to their encounter with the Jesuits, just as a multiplicity of Native
viewpoints exists in Canada today. Many people within the same
community, even the same family, were divided in their assessment
of the priests and in their ideas about how best to deal with them,
and these points of view changed over time.

In addition, while colonial discourses can be shown to have used
similar themes and strategies, the nature of these themes varied

considerably over time and space. Accounts written by early-sixteenth-century explorers, for whom the world was still populated by bizarre and monstrous forms of humanity, and those written by the nineteenth-century administrators of colonial India intent on implementing a system of rational rule, for example, were distinctly different. There is a risk of fetishizing colonialism and its discourses in a way that reduces it to a single monolithic process.

The Jesuits wrote before the European Enlightenment, and their portrayal of North America did not rely on the themes of reason and progress which formed part of the ideological architecture of modernity and which were so important in the colonial discourses representing the "primitive" throughout the eighteenth, nineteenth, and twentieth centuries. In addition, at the time the Jesuits wrote, neither the cultures of early modern Europe nor their respective members shared a single set of meanings and purposes. The discourses of discovery and exploration were primarily the product of a ruling elite whose point of view was not necessarily shared by the variety of ordinary men and women who lived in the New World or Europe (Greenblatt 1991, 146). The emerging national boundaries of seventeenth-century Europe encompassed a variety of interests, and the aims of the French who came to and traded in the St Lawrence region were by no means one and the same. The goals of the Jesuits and other missionaries were not those of individual traders, many of whom opposed French settlement and the disruption of Aboriginal economies, which threatened to be among the consequences of the missions. The Jesuits were frequently frustrated by the behaviour of some of the traders and interpreters who had preceded them to North America, either because their behaviour was – in the Jesuits' view – immoral or because it introduced indigenous people to the complicating alternatives of Protestantism. The Jesuits' desire to create new and orthodox Christians in the context of a reformed Catholicism, as well as their ambition to recreate the religious unity of pre-Reformation Europe, was made more difficult by the impossibility of any such uniformity or general orthodoxy in the larger French population.

My discussion of the Jesuits, other French, and the Native people who interacted in the St Lawrence region in the first half of the seventeenth century is thus not undertaken to reduce either Europeans or Native peoples to definitive and discrete categories, cultures, or otherwise homogeneous orders. As a religious order, the

Society of Jesus did advocate general policies and objectives. These
will be useful to refer to in the course of this analysis, especially
since the *Relations* themselves were produced as official publications and represented the public face of the order more than
individual differences within it. However, like any organization, no
less than any conventionally defined culture, the existence of apparent institutional norms belied the extent of individual variation and
internal conflict. In the case of Aboriginal people, while I refer to
those aspects of their ways of life that were relevant to their
interaction with the Jesuits, I will treat these as characteristics of
groups of people who were involved in ongoing symbolic, economic, and political processes, both internally and in relationship
with others, and who continued to be so involved after the arrival
of the French.

   While the classic anthropological approach to culture initially
emphasized the distinctiveness of cultural wholes, as well as their
relative worth, this approach did little to account for historical
change and the innovations that occurred as a result of the interaction between people from differing cultures. Indeed, these border-
land areas were formerly understood to be the sites of contamination
of authentic tradition rather than the sites of cultural production
(Rosaldo 1989, 28). The language of culture clash, contact, and
even loss reflects this idea of cultures as discrete wholes. Critics of
this model of culture have identified it as static and objectifying,
tending to freeze cultures in time while denying the connections
between them, and they have argued that cultures are neither such
discrete islands nor even unified and interpretable systems of symbols and meanings (Wolf 1982, 18; Clifford 1986, 19). This book
is informed by an understanding of culture as a mutable, shifting,
and historically constituted result of shared but unbounded social
experiences, practices, and meanings "in which power is always
implicated" (Comaroff and Comaroff 1991, 313). To approach
culture in this way does not deny real differences between the way
people construct the world, or the fact that symbolic invention is
integral to human existence and social life, as well as to the projects
of colonialism and resistance to it. This approach does, however,
attempt to avoid the objectification of these differences that occurs
when cultures are written about as permanent and knowable entities; seeing cultures in this way has been an integral component of
colonial knowledge.

OUTLINE

The following chapter provides a brief introduction to the Jesuits and their missions among the people they knew as the Huron and Montagnais. I situate the Jesuits' arrival in North America in the context of the prevailing religious, political, and economic climate in France, and the interests this climate either generated or failed to generate in North America. I also introduce the broad parameters of the Jesuits' establishment of their missions among the Montagnais and Huron, and the social and economic factors that influenced their approach to these missions.

Chapter 3 explores the Jesuits' interpretation of the Aboriginal inhabitants of northeastern North America as the savage occupants of a barren and hostile land. The physical and spiritual qualities of the wilderness and their implications for the condition of those who lived in it are discussed in relation to the imperatives of the Christian mission and the Jesuits' representation of this mission according to agrarian metaphors of domestication and harvest. The Jesuits described a state of savagery that included an assemblage of traits and knowable features. Their descriptions were influenced by a biblical philosophy of degeneration as well as by folkloric images of the Wild Man. The Wild Man was originally human but lived beyond the pale of civilization and had been reduced, as a result of this, to the condition of brutes. The state of savagery which the Jesuits created in their *Relations* also included being lost to history, and the priests suggested that Aboriginal people could be brought out of this condition of absence through their own saving agency.

Among the features that distinguished the savage from the civil was the presence or absence of mechanisms for the maintenance of social order, including the ability of leaders to punish transgressors and to demand obedience from their subjects. These had not been absent in other areas of Jesuit missions, such as India, China, and Japan. Chapter 4 deals with the implications of the Jesuits' assumptions about law and order in northeastern North America, where authority was understood quite differently, and it examines the attempts made by the priests and other French officials to impose what they considered more appropriate legal and governing procedures. The Jesuits did come to understand Aboriginal processes of legal resolution and even went so far as to defend their effectiveness in relative terms. However, I situate the priests' ultimate emphasis on establishing more coercive mechanisms of law and punishment in Aboriginal communities in the context of their belief that the full comprehension of the duties of Christianity depended on a corresponding comprehension of the necessity of obedience.

I return to the themes of obedience, humility, and punishment in chapter 5 in connection with the Jesuits' interpretation of the causes of infectious diseases among Aboriginal populations. The priests represented these diseases as either divine punishment resulting from people's continued resistance to Christianity or as trials sent to test and strengthen the faith of new converts. The Jesuits further rationalized the suffering and loss of life resulting from these diseases by employing a recuperative logic, whereby to lose all was to gain all and to suffer in this life was, generally, to reap more benefits in the next life. While the Jesuits were dogmatic in their assertions, both in the pages of the *Relations* and in their arguments with Aboriginal people suffering the diseases, they themselves were vigorously accused of causing the diseases through witchcraft. The Jesuits and Native people both interpreted the diseases in such a way that the behaviour of the other in each case was seen as damning proof and justification for the validity of their own interpretation. In the *Relations*, however, the Jesuits had the last word and were able to argue that, in the New World, disease taught Christian humility in a way that political authority could not.

CHAPTER TWO

Jesuit Beginnings
in New France

D'aller partout ... chez les fidèles ou les infidèles, sans alléguer d'excuse
et sans demander aucune provision de route, pour les affaires qui concernent
le culte divin et le bien de la religion chrétienne.

Ignatius Loyola, *Constitutions of the Society of Jesus*

The first Jesuits arrived in northeastern North America in 1611.[1]
During the summer of that year, Fathers Pierre Biard and Enemond
Massé accompanied Jean de Biencourt de Poutrincourt to the small,
recently established settlement of Port-Royal, in what is now Nova
Scotia. Samuel de Champlain had established Port-Royal as a settlement in 1605, and it was subsequently given to Poutrincourt as
a seigneury. After Biard and Massé arrived, Poutrincourt returned
to France, and relations between the two priests and his son, whom
he had left in charge at Port-Royal, deteriorated. The situation was
not improved when Poutrincourt lost the favour of the Jesuits'
influential sponsor, Madame la Marquise de Guercheville. The
marquise decided to remove the Jesuits from Port-Royal, and in
1613, after Biard and Massé had been joined by Brother Gilbert
Du Thet and Father Jacques Quentin, they chose a new site on the
island of St-Sauveur off the coast of what is now Maine. They had
barely begun this new establishment when Samuel Argall arrived
from the English colony of Virginia with the intention of asserting,
with cannon, the rights of England over the region. The French
were taken by surprise and forced to surrender. Father Massé
escaped and found passage back to France on a fishing ship, Biard
and Quentin were taken captive but eventually returned to France,
and Du Thet was killed by an English volley while trying to aim and
fire a cannon. Argall compelled Biard to accompany him to Port-Royal,
and for this Poutrincourt's supporters denounced Biard as a traitor.
After these events, anti-Jesuit sentiments prevailed and general
opinion was for keeping the Jesuits out of New France.

At the time of Biard's and Massé's arrival in North America, the Society of Jesus had existed as a religious order for less than a century, having been founded by Ignatius Loyola in 1534 and confirmed by a papal bull in 1540. Martin Luther had nailed his ninety-five theses to the door at Wittenberg only twenty-three years before this confirmation, and the first Jesuits took their vows in the midst of a politically and religiously divided Europe. While Loyola did not initiate the society as a direct response to the Protestant Reformation (O'Malley 1993, 18, 278), he did envision it in such a way that it came to be effective in the Catholic reform that followed the challenge of Luther and the spread of Protestantism. One of Loyola's most significant innovations was his rejection of the monastic model, in which individual monks sought their own salvation away from the world, and his stipulation that Jesuits perform an active ministry in the world, working for the salvation of others (Martin 1988, 26–8).[2] He combined this purpose with a desire to emulate the original apostles of Christ, resulting in the distinct shape and content of the Jesuits' ministry – the teaching, itinerant preaching, and mission work through which the Jesuits distinguished themselves and defined their order (O'Malley 1993, 18).[3] Missionary work among non-Christians abroad and among Catholics closer to home who had become or were at risk of becoming Protestant was a direct corollary of this apostolic model which motivated Loyola and his early companions and became a central activity of the order. The Jesuits also expressed this missionary vocation in a fourth vow, which they took in addition to the vows of poverty, obedience, and chastity, stating their willingness to go wherever the present or future pontiff chose to send them for the propagation of the faith.

Many Jesuits initially excelled in missions in the European countryside, where they worked to educate the peasantry in Catholicism and to ward off the threat of Protestant ascendancy. Historians are in general agreement, and not without cause, on the success of the society in this role (e.g., Olin 1969, 198; Evennett 1958, 300; Kidd 1963, 39; Russell 1946, 545). While the Jesuits have been popularized as the shock troops of the Counter-Reformation, it is not overstating the case to say that they played a significant role in the pastoral reforms implemented during this time and that they were active in the defence and propagation of the Roman Catholic faith in Europe and abroad (O'Malley 1993, 18). The vindictive attacks on the order by Protestant writers throughout Europe are themselves persuasive evidence of the threat the Jesuits posed to the growth of Protestantism (Martin 1973, 17).

That the Jesuits were so successful as missionaries is partially attributable to the innovative and occasionally controversial policies they employed. These included a willingness to accommodate the popular forms of devotion that were characteristic of the countryside and a recognition that reform would be most effective if it acknowledged the needs of the average parishioner (Briggs 1989, 351–2). The Jesuits adopted this approach in their missions outside Europe as well and, in doing so, demonstrated a tolerance of local custom that often earned them criticism at home. Loyola had purposely combined the emphasis on itinerant missions with the recommendation that Jesuits adapt what they said and did to whatever circumstances they were confronted with (O'Malley 1993, 255) – in short, being all things to all people. This technique was part of their "way of proceeding" (ibid.) and had been used by Jesuit missionaries in Japan, China, India, and South America before the order's arrival in northeastern North America.

The North American mission offered new opportunities for the fulfilment of the ideal of arduous propagation of the faith which inspired many Jesuits. This motivation was perhaps more acute in the first half of the seventeenth century, for it was during this time that France was the scene of the intense spirituality that marked the final and most emphatic stage of the Counter-Reformation (Church 1972, 40). An intensified concern for all things religious prevailed among the educated classes, the Catholic clergy, and at court. The period was characterized by institutional reforms and increased support for missions, both foreign and domestic, as well as an intensification of devotion that ranged from individual mysticism to concerted attempts on the part of devotional organizations to implement rigorous, and in some cases oppressive, standards of public morality.

The Jesuits participated in the devotional emphasis of this period and benefited from it; Biard and Massé's first passage to North America was financed in the context of the heightened support for missions that was characteristic of the time. However, the Jesuits' missionary tactics, both at home and abroad, were not always consistent with the more absolute ideals of those who were caught up in the devotional emphasis. The elite clergy in particular decried the religious practices and morality of ordinary parishioners as obstacles to reform and to the practice of true religion (Briggs 1986, 10–11). They and others supported rural missions because they wanted these apparently superstitious and irreligious practices replaced with more uniform and orthodox forms of devotion. The overseas missions that gained favour at this time were supported for similar reasons.

The Jesuits' approach to their missionary work reflected their humanistic emphasis as well as their earlier engagement with the teachings of Thomas Aquinas on grace and nature. Loyola and the first members of the Jesuit order had embraced Aquinas's position on these issues in the sixteenth century. The position on grace and nature taken by the Catholic Church during the Council of Trent also reflected Aquinas's teachings. Aquinas had argued that God's grace was available to all people and that because human will had not been entirely obliterated by original sin, it could cooperate with grace and so be active in salvation; in this view, grace perfected nature (O'Malley 1993, 249). Catholic orthodoxy had generally taken the position that God gave all humans, including pagans, help in the form of grace to perform meritorious actions (Brockliss 1987, 249). The Jesuits in the seventeenth century held to this relatively generous view of human nature, and to the possibility of achieving God's grace, at a time when the more severe Augustinian theology – according to which original sin had left human nature more thoroughly corrupted – was gaining favour in France. The Jansenists, with whom the Jesuits were in frequent conflict toward the mid and latter portions of the seventeenth century, reflected this spirit of severity in their rejection of the possibility that non-Christians could perform moral or meritorious acts, or have any innate knowledge of God. Statements in the *Relations*, such as that written by Jérôme Lalemant in 1647 to the effect that "it is certain that all men are created in order to know, to love, and to enjoy their God; all have the means to do this, but very diversely" speak directly to this debate and amplify the Jesuits' position (31:231).

Thus, although the Jesuits shared some of the objectives of the morally rigorous *devots*, they differed in the extent to which they were prepared to step back from the absolute standards of the time and acknowledge the realities of human frailty, both as missionaries and as confessors. This did not necessarily represent the spiritual commitment of individual Jesuits, however, which was just as likely to take an intense, mystical, or rigorous form. In spite of these differences, the Jesuits and *devots* were united in encouraging support for both domestic and foreign missions, as well as for the elimination of Protestantism from France, by military means if necessary. Although the Edict of Nantes had guaranteed French Protestants a degree of religious freedom in 1598, many Catholics continued to support an ideal of doctrinal unity that rejected any such tolerance. Missions to the New World offered the Jesuits and other missionaries the opportunity to reestablish the ideal of an uncontested Catholic Christianity and to reclaim some of the former prestige of the Catholic Church. The influence of Protestant traders in the St Lawrence and the presence of northern European Protestants on the eastern coast of North America threatened this opportunity and contributed significantly to the missionary zeal of individual Jesuits.

The religious motivations of the Jesuits and the *devots* notwithstanding, missions to North America were not possible without interests in trade and exploration and the ability of the parties interested in these ventures to sustain them. In North America as elsewhere, missionaries followed commerce, finding their wealth in souls at the same time as traders and merchants found wealth in commodities. The colonial endeavours of France had not yet been as successful as those of the Spanish, Dutch, or English in either settlement or trade. This has been attributed to a number of factors, including deficiencies in shipbuilding and navigation, a comparably lower level of development in industry, and competition among independent trading companies such as those that operated on the St Lawrence (Lublinskaya 1968, 144–5). Smaller companies located in competing urban centres were in frequent conflict with the trading companies that sought monopoly interests in the St Lawrence valley, and they often continued to compete, illegally, for the fur trade even when monopolies were granted to other companies.

The mercantilist logic of the day supported the involvement of a strong and centralized government in overseas trade and the development of colonies as markets for domestic manufactures. However, the French government tended to see much more commercial potential in the exploitable resources of the West Indies than in northeastern North America. There was also little incentive for settlement. Although the fur trade on the St Lawrence was profitable, the companies involved in it did not generally favour bringing over colonists. They did not need settlers for the pursuit of the trade and in fact viewed them as potential competitors for furs (Trigger 1985, 307). The conditions of the monopolies granted by the crown in the early seventeenth century invariably required companies to take measures to promote and finance settlement, but these conditions were only minimally complied with, both because of an absence of will on the part of the companies and because of very real financial and logistical difficulties that had to be overcome in meeting such conditions.

Samuel de Champlain, whose involvement in the St Lawrence region spanned the first third of the century, was particularly interested in the establishment of self-sustaining French settlements there. He also advocated the introduction of Christianity to the Native people who were trading with the French. Champlain was a colony builder more than a trader, and he undertook numerous initiatives to promote colonization, engaging the mercantilist spirit of the times while describing the benefits of concentrated interest in North America. He did not, however, achieve the success he hoped for. The pursuit of his agenda brought him into conflict with the more pragmatic interests of the traders (Trigger 1985, 319), for neither settlement nor wholesale attempts to change the way Native peoples lived, much less their religious beliefs, were at that time advantageous from the perspective of profitable trade. Interests in profit in the context of emerging capitalism, and interests in the spiritual welfare of non-Christians in the context of the devout religiosity of the seventeenth century were uneasily conjoined in New France. This was partly because of the mixture of Protestant and Catholic interests in the trading companies, on whose support missionaries often depended.

Champlain independently raised funds to bring four Recollet friars, of the Order of Friars Minor, to Quebec in 1615. The Recollets came to Canada with the verbal permission of the Holy See, and although this was made official by a papal charter in 1618, they were not at any time given exclusive rights to the Canadian mission. They expressed a very poor view of the character, religious capacity, and way of life of the Aboriginal people they encountered, and they were not very successful in winning converts to Christianity. They did, however, actively support Champlain in his vision of settlement and the development of the St Lawrence region as a French and exclusively Catholic colony.

The Jesuits joined the Recollets on the St Lawrence in July 1625, when Fathers Jean de Brébeuf, Charles Lalemant, and Enemond Massé arrived at Quebec. Massé had spent the years after his expulsion from St-Sauveur teaching at the Jesuit college at La Flèche in northern France, all the while working toward just such a return to North America. He had communicated his zeal for overseas missionary work to a number of his pupils at the college, where missions to North America were considered an ideal opportunity for the pursuit of rigorous asceticism and self-sacrifice (Pouliot 1966, 453). Although the Recollets had had very little success in converting anybody to Christianity, it is not clear that they really wanted the Jesuits' help or approved of their sudden appearance in the colony. The Jesuits owed their arrival to the backing of the new and devoutly Catholic viceroy of New France, the Duc de Ventadour, who personally financed the passages for Brébeuf, Lalemant, and Massé (Trigger 1987, 494). A few years later Ventadour founded the Compagnie du Saint-Sacrament, a secret society whose objectives included the maintenance of rigorous forms of Catholic devotion as well as the elimination of Protestantism in France (Maland 1970, 178; Trigger 1985, 325). His religious zeal was extreme, and the compagnie can be seen as one of the more repressive manifestations of the religious enthusiasm of the period. For their part, the Jesuits involved had effectively engaged Ventadour's religious fervour in a way that ensured them a measure of political protection in North America.[4]

The Jesuits' first arrival at Quebec also coincided with the increasing interest of the French government under the aegis of Cardinal Richelieu, first minister to Louis XIII, in questions of trade. In 1627 Richelieu oversaw the replacement of the existing trading monopoly of the de Caën group, whose principals included both Catholics and Protestants, with a monopoly granted to the Company of One Hundred Associates, also known as the Company of New France. The associates of this company were to be exclusively Catholic, to the satisfaction of the Jesuits and Recollets.

Richelieu's interest in trade did not initiate a period of prosperity and settlement in New France, nor did it lead to financial backing from the French government. The Company of One Hundred Associates suffered considerable losses in its first years, and the English occupation of Quebec prevented it from trading at all between 1629 and 1632. It was not until 1663, under the efforts of

Jean-Baptiste Colbert in his capacity as first minister to Louis XIV, that trade and settlement in North America received financial support from the royal treasury of France.

Richelieu's attention to the economic potential of trade in North America and elsewhere was related to his program of state building in France. He looked to the colonies and their resources in order to strengthen the state financially. The consolidation of France as a state occurred, like other European states, in concert with developments in overseas trade, colonial expansion, and commercial capitalism (Wallerstein 1974, 133). These were the same processes that were the infrastructure of much mission work around the globe. Specifically, Richelieu's immediate concern with trade was as a measure to enhance royal finances in order to support his objective of suppressing, with force, the political and military powers of the French Protestants, the Huguenots. The Huguenots were an organized force that included a number of free towns as well as prominent nobles and princes of the blood. Richelieu and other advocates of a strong and central monarchy thought that the political and military independence of these Protestants, including their right to maintain fortified towns, conflicted with the process of centralizing authority in the French crown, which had begun in the preceding century (Lublinskaya 1968, 148, 169).

The Huguenot party was also a vehicle for the expression of dissatisfaction by nobles who were intent on preserving their feudal privileges at the expense of centralization. This dissatisfaction had already played a significant role in the wars that had plagued France during the last half of the sixteenth century. Although these wars – which should be understood as both civil and religious – were now over, many of the advocates of Catholic reform continued to argue for the suppression of the Huguenots on religious grounds and in this way actively supported the government's action. Richelieu's policies ultimately disappointed the *devots* no less than the Jesuits, for although the military campaigns against the Huguenots were successful, the defeat of cities such as La Rochelle did not require the elimination of freedom of worship as a condition of surrender; the outcome was simply the destruction of all fortifications and a reduction in the rights that had been guaranteed in the Edict of Nantes and its amendments (ibid., 168, 219).

The Jesuits who left France for North America in the first half of the seventeenth century thus did so in the context of an increasingly centralized and absolutist monarchy. While absolutism suggests tyranny, in both practice and in theory it was more limited than the term implies and should be understood in comparison with the division of power among lesser lords that was characteristic of feudalism; an absolute monarch replaced this previous "scattering" of power (Wallerstein 1974, 144).[5] Nevertheless, the emphasis on order and authority that permeated political and social thought at this time is of particular relevance when considered in relation to the priests' impression of North America.

Absolutism combined a long tradition of belief in the mystical properties and sacred character of French kingship with political arguments that increased the extent and legitimate uses of sovereign power (Church 1972, 27). Absolutist theory emphasized the role of the sovereign not only as the ultimate source of authority in the state but as the ordering principle that held the polity together (Keohane 1980, 17). The elaboration of the king as the image of God on earth included a parallel between the power of the king to act as a unifying and regulating force within the realm, and the power of God's will to fashion and then regulate the universe (ibid.). The metaphor of the polity as a body – the *corps mystique* – with the king serving symbolically as the head, ordering and regulating the various orders and estates, also had a long history in French political thought. In the context of absolutism, the degree of authority of the king as the head, as well as the need for order and obedience within the component parts that made up the realm, was intensified, while the concept of order within an integrated whole remained. Richelieu's own arguments in support of absolutism referred to the necessary subordination of the varying elements of the social order, including the clergy, nobility, and peasantry, as the component parts of the state (ibid., 179).

When this interchanging metaphor of body and polity was continued in philosophy and theology, individuals were envisaged as miniature body politics, composed of potentially disruptive passions and desires that had to be ordered and submitted to the sovereignty of reason, as well as to the external guidance provided by social institutions and the state (ibid., 451). In their policies, the Jesuits in general promoted a more positive relationship between passions and reason than other moralists did, particularly the Jansenists (Brockliss 1987, 173). Even so, their association between the indulgence of physical appetites and sin and the necessity of restraining and overcoming these appetites, long a feature of Christianity, showed up in stark contrast in North America. In political theory, the sovereign power was itself encompassed by regulatory forces and institutions, or "bridles," which contributed to order within the realm through their enforcement but which also, ideally, existed to check the abuse of sovereign power and the disintegration of governance into the free play of the king's personal passions. I shall return to the issue of bridles in connection with social order in chapter 4, where I show it to be of particular significance in the interpretation of law, or its absence, in North America. The emphasis on order and obedience within the individual and between individuals as members of social estates, as well as the relationship of this to both individual salvation and the creation of a larger social order that promoted salvation in general, will also be seen in the Jesuits' reactions to the social and political organizations of the peoples they encountered in North America.

When Richelieu launched a military campaign against the Huguenot city of La Rochelle, the English, under Charles I and the Duke of Buckingham, decided to support the Protestants, and the siege led to a minor war between France and England. This in turn resulted in the loss of the fort of Quebec in 1629, for it provided justification for the English to attempt to drive the French from the St Lawrence and seize the fur trade. After Champlain surrendered Quebec in the spring of that year, the Jesuits and Recollets had to abandon the mission and return to France. The war was of relatively short duration, and England returned Quebec to France in the spring of 1632. Champlain and the Company of One Hundred Associates then began plans to resume trade and reoccupy Quebec. A monopoly on souls was as important as a monopoly on trade, and the Jesuits set about securing exclusive missionary rights to the colony at the expense of the Recollets. They were supported by Jean de Lauson, the intendant of the Company of One Hundred Associates. Cardinal Richelieu's adviser at this time was the Capuchin Father Joseph, and he encouraged the cardinal to pass over both the Recollets and the Jesuits and assign the mission to his own order. Lauson, however, managed to convince the Capuchins to limit their evangelical pursuits in New France to the eastern coast and to help him persuade Richelieu to assign the rest of the colony to the Jesuits. Although the Recollets bitterly opposed these decisions, their complaints of unfair treatment were ignored by Lauson.

The Jesuits successfully secured the monopoly and remained the only missionaries on the St Lawrence until 1657. Fathers Paul Le Jeune and Anne de Noüe set sail from Dieppe on 18 April 1632 and arrived at Quebec on 5 July. They were joined the following year by the returning Fathers Brébeuf and Massé, as well as by Fathers Antoine Daniel and Ambroise Davost. Father Le Jeune was the first superior of the Jesuit mission at Quebec and continued in that position until 1639, when he was replaced by Barthélemy Vimont. Born of Protestant parents, Le Jeune had converted to Roman Catholicism as a youth, entering the novitiate of the Society of Jesus at Paris in 1613. Unlike many others who came to New France as missionaries, Le Jeune had not previously expressed an interest in doing so (Pouliot 1966, 453). He had, however, been among the pupils at La Flèche who were exposed to Enemond Massé's unquenchable zeal for the New France mission (Trigger 1987, 472). In his tenure as superior, Le Jeune combined practicality with zeal, and he remained connected with the Jesuit missions in New France until just before his death in 1664. As the superior at Quebec he wrote the annual *Relation* from 1632 until 1639, and he continued to write it, on behalf of Vimont, until 1642. Le Jeune returned to France in 1649 and assumed the position of procurator of the Canadian missions; in this capacity he continued to oversee, edit, and in some cases contribute to the *Relations* (Pouliot 1966, 454).

THE MISSIONS

The analysis in this book covers the *Relations* that were written between 1632 and 1650, during which time the Jesuits' missions were primarily among peoples the French knew as the Huron and Montagnais.[6] The term Montagnais did not refer to one single political entity but encompassed a number of small organized groups that inhabited the north shore of the St Lawrence River and spread well into the interior. By the time Le Jeune arrived in 1632, the majority of the Montagnais on the north shore already had considerable experience of trading with Europeans, dating back to the voyages of Jacques Cartier (Bailey 1969, 35). Those resident in the area of Tadoussac occupied an especially strategic position at the mouth of the Saguenay River, which emptied into the St Lawrence, and had been engaged as middlemen between their

northern neighbours and European fur traders at least as early as
1599 (Trigger 1987, 213). By the beginning of the seventeenth
century, French traders had realized the importance of securing a
stable trading relationship with the Montagnais who had access to
the most promising fur resources to the north of the St Lawrence
(ibid., 229). It was partly because of this that the French expressed
a willingness to participate in the wars of their Montagnais trading
partners and their allies, whose conflicts at that time were primarily
with members of the Iroquois confederacy to the south.[7] The
French knew that military assistance was one of the most effective
ways of gaining the confidence and trust of Aboriginal trading
partners, so they agreed to participate in these wars in order to
protect and expand their fur trade (Trigger 1985, 175).

Trading relations among Native people in the Northeast at this
time involved complex reciprocal social and political obligations,
including military alliances. For Native people, trade with Europeans was desirable for the material items it provided, but these were
means to greater ends in societies where prestige and status were
largely associated with generosity and the ability to give away
wealth. While French and other European traders engaged in trade
in a social, political, and economic context that made its pursuit
meaningful to them, Aboriginal people not only did the same, but
they brought their expectations to bear on the conduct of the
Europeans who wished to establish trade relationships. These relationships were not ones in which Europeans quickly assumed dominance and easily exploited Aboriginal people (Francis and Morantz
1983, 167–8; see also Ray 1974, 61).

Champlain's agreement to assume the military obligations of a
trading ally brought the French into a long-standing conflict with
the Iroquois, but it was consistent with the expectations of the
Montagnais and other Aboriginal people toward the French as
trading partners. Champlain fulfilled these obligations by accompanying a number of Montagnais and Algonkin men up the Richelieu River into what is now New York State, where they fought a
party of approximately two hundred Iroquois warriors.[8] The presence of Champlain and two other Frenchmen, armed with muskets,
was instrumental in the success of this campaign, though the Iroquois against whom they fought later used European arms to
distinct advantage. A small number of Huron men accompanied
this expedition on the invitation of their Algonkin allies. This

resulted in the first direct contact between French and Huron people in North America (Heidenreich 1971, 233–4).

The subsistence economy of the Montagnais featured importantly in their relationship with the Jesuits, figuring in the priests' initial assessment of the quality of their life, their social and political organization, and what had to be done to convert them to Christianity. In the early seventeenth century, this economy involved a seasonal round of hunting, gathering, and fishing, the primary feature of which was the removal of groups of three to four families from the shores of the St Lawrence in the fall in order to hunt moose and caribou inland during the winter. These groups later returned to the banks of the river, where larger numbers of people congregated during spring and summer. The winter portion of these activities are vividly detailed in Le Jeune's *Relation* of 1634. Le Jeune spent the winter of 1633–34 travelling with three brothers and their families, hoping that by doing so he might learn the language and begin the religious instruction of his hosts. The brothers included Pierre Pastedechouan, who could speak French and who Le Jeune hoped would act as a translator; Mestigoit, whom Le Jeune identified as the leader of the group; and a shaman by the name of Carigonan. Pierre had been taken to France by the Recollets in 1620, where he had received Christian instruction and baptism and been taught to speak and write in both French and Latin (Grassmann 1966, 533).[9] He returned to North America with the Recollets in 1626 but eventually gave up Christianity. When Le Jeune accompanied this family, they spent the winter inland from the south shore of the St Lawrence River, opposite Tadoussac. The Montagnais used the hunting territories south of the St Lawrence less and less during the next decade. Although these areas were more productive, hunting there became too dangerous, for it exposed people to the risk of attack by Iroquois raiding parties (Bailey 1969, 35).

Le Jeune devoted considerable commentary in his *Relation* to the ritual and religious observances that he witnessed over the winter, including the care taken in the disposal of animal bones and other remains. The respectful treatment of animal remains was part of a more comprehensive set of rituals surrounding hunting, all of which were of primary importance in ensuring its continued success (Speck 1935, 77). Hunting was not just a matter of skill; it occurred in the context of mutual relationships between humans and animals. These were complex, culturally determined relationships, which were the result neither of a way of life that had more in common with that of beasts than humans, as suggested by many of the Jesuits, nor of a natural, premodern, ecological sensitivity, as is sometimes implied in popular interpretations of Native cultures. Animals cooperated in the hunt by allowing themselves to be killed, but their souls, which were equal in all senses to those of human beings, remained to observe the way in which their remains were treated (ibid.). The observances Le Jeune took to be isolated and meaningless, devoid of the awe and ceremony attendant to the performance of Christian ritual, were integral to the maintenance of these relationships.

Other ritual activities observed by Le Jeune included the singing, drumming, and divination carried out by members of the group, especially Carigonan. As the men and women who were most successful at obtaining spiritual power, shamans frequently assisted others in their capacity as healers and diviners (Rogers and Leacock 1981, 184). Le Jeune witnessed the performance of a shaking tent ceremony conducted by Carigonan for the purpose of forecasting hunting success and the health of members of the group (6:167–9). In another instance, Carigonan pitted his energies against a distant but rival shaman and claimed to have caused his death. This was done in spite of Le Jeune's attempts to teach the Christian commandment against killing, and it could have been partially motivated as a show of power intended to impress or at least intimidate the priest (6:199). The common use of spiritual power for both altruistic and hostile purposes differed considerably from Le Jeune's Christian assumption of an exclusive opposition between good and evil. Similarly, the participatory role of the shaman as an active and not necessarily submissive agent in manipulating the effects of spiritual power was unlike the position of either the priest or the parishioner in Christianity. In any case, Le Jeune did not believe that the shaman had access to the forces he himself would have understood as evil, much less anything else (6:199–201). Le Jeune characterized all the ritual activities and religious beliefs that he observed during the winter as superstitions, and he attempted to disprove them to his hosts, either empirically or by argument, a feat that was complicated by his lack of proficiency in the language. Despite this disadvantage, he tried to discredit Carigonan's authority as much as possible, and the two men spent the winter in a state of undisguised hostility and rivalry (7:61).

While Le Jeune continually accused the shaman of falsehood and chicanery, he himself was the frequent subject of teasing and banter bordering on ridicule, both from Carigonan and from other members of the three families (7:61). The priest ruefully admitted an unexpected familiarity with the language of insults, if nothing else, after the winter was over (ibid.).[10] The teasing arose from the poor opinion the people had of Le Jeune's behaviour and physical appearance. They found his beard, like those of most Europeans, especially unattractive (7:63), but they also teased him in an attempt to pressure him into greater compliance with their ideas about how to behave. This type of teasing was useful in a situation where no individual had the authority to forbid or dictate the actions of anyone else (Leacock 1981, 191).

The Jesuits eventually viewed the relative importance of individual autonomy that was a feature of Montagnais social relations as incompatible with Christian norms and an impediment to the success of the mission. The fluidity of Montagnais social groupings and the demonstrable absence of coercive mechanisms of social and political regulation contributed to these views. However, the priests were initially more concerned about the Montagnais' hunting, fishing, and gathering economy, both because they interpreted it as an unstable and vulnerable way of life and because its non-sedentary nature made attempts at conversion logistically difficult. Le Jeune returned from his winter journey exhausted and discouraged, little further ahead in the language, and convinced, like the Recollets before him, that the only way to convert these people was to encourage their settlement. He subsequently directed considerable attention to the establishment of a permanent Christian village for Montagnais families near Quebec. Although such a village was eventually established, it was not as effective as Le Jeune had envisioned and was eventually abandoned; but many Montagnais continued to be ministered to by a few missionaries who travelled with them during the winter.

After Le Jeune's return from his travels in the winter of 1633–34, the Jesuits placed their greatest hope for success with the more sedentary Huron people, who were then living in a small area just east of Georgian Bay in what is now southern Ontario. The Huron economy was based on corn agriculture, supplemented by some fishing, hunting, and gathering, as well as trade. As indicated above, Huron traders did not become involved in direct relationships with

French traders until the first decade of the seventeenth century, but they had had indirect access to European trade goods before then, primarily through the Algonkin peoples living to their east, in the area of the Ottawa River Valley (Biggar [1922–36] 1971, 1:164). A number of these Algonkin groups had recognized the strategic advantage of their position between the French in the St Lawrence and the Huron in the interior, and had unsuccessfully tried to preserve their position as middlemen in the fur trade by preventing direct contact between these two peoples (Day and Trigger 1978, 793). Traders and missionaries had to travel through Algonkin territory on their way to and from Huron country. The Kichesipirini Algonkin, situated on Morrisson's Island in the Ottawa River, had initially refused to allow Champlain passage beyond the island to the Nipissing, who were the closest neighbours of the Huron (Biggar [1922–36] 1971, 2:285–8). Even after Champlain and the Huron had concluded a trading alliance, the Kichesipirini delayed Huron traders on their way to the St Lawrence, exacting payment from them before allowing them to continue their journey (Heidenreich 1971, 263). Much of the direct trade which the Huron conducted with the French relied on previously existing trading relations with the Huron's more northerly and fur-rich Algonkian-speaking neighbours, from whom they obtained furs in exchange for corn and European trade goods (Tooker [1964] 1991, 25).

Population estimates for the Huron in the early seventeenth century are between eighteen and forty thousand people, distributed in eighteen to twenty-five villages (Trigger 1987, 32). At the time the Jesuits began their mission among them, the Huron were organized into a four-member confederacy that included the Attignawantan, Attigneenongnahac, Arendarhonon, and Tahontaenrat. Of these, the Attignawantan were the most numerous and prominent, occupying up to fourteen villages and representing approximately half of the Huron population (Tooker [1964] 1991, 11). While the Jesuits attributed a higher degree of civil organization to the Huron than to the Montagnais, they were frustrated by the dispersal of authority among Huron leaders. In the villages, the Jesuits encountered headmen who represented the clan segments within the village; each clan segment chose one headman for civil affairs and one for the affairs of war, and it was these civil leaders who together acted as village headmen and organized the village councils (Trigger 1987, 56). However, none of these headmen had the power to command any other. Beyond the villages, each member of the confederacy designated a leader from among the village headmen, but although this leader represented a larger political entity, his principal sphere of influence remained that of his own clan segment (ibid., 57).

The designation of leaders relied in part on matrilineal principles of descent, a situation in obvious contrast to the emphasis on heredity through the male line among the nobility in France. In each case, the men who stood to assume leadership positions by virtue of kinship were also assessed on the basis of their personal qualifications; they had to be proficient warriors, generous, intelligent, and very well spoken (ibid., 55). Generosity and the willingness to subordinate their own interests to the interests of the community were especially important (Sioui 1994, 289). On the selection of leaders, Brébeuf wrote: "They reach this degree of honor, partly through succession, partly through election; their children do not usually succeed them, but properly their nephews and grandsons. And the latter do not even come to the succession of these petty Royalties, like the Dauphins of France, or children to the inheritance of their fathers; but only in so far as they have suitable qualification, and accept the position, and are accepted by the whole Country" (10:233).

While Huron men were the most visible figures in public affairs, women had considerable influence in community affairs, contrary to the assumption of the priests and other early European observers (Trigger 1985, 89). Decisions in councils were made through a process of debate leading to consensus, although the Jesuits noted that the opinions of the eldest men and the leaders were the most influential in directing that consensus (10:251). Headmen displayed their rhetorical skills in these councils, and the Jesuits did not fail to comment positively on how eloquently and persuasively many of them spoke. The confederacy council appears to have met once a year (Sagard [1939] 1968, 150) or when there was an emergency. In at least one case, such a meeting was called to discuss the future of the relationship between the Huron and the Jesuits. Although members of the confederacy shared common interests and a similar way of life, they did not always agree on the issues affecting them, nor did they act entirely as one body.

The Jesuits initially believed that the Huron did not have an organized religious system of their own and would therefore be easy to convert. The priests came to this conclusion after noting an absence of the kind of institutionalized structures and practices that were characteristic of the religions they were familiar with, such as Christianity, Islam, and Judaism. It was only after they had devoted considerably more time and effort to the attempt to convert people that the Jesuits realized the extent to which religious beliefs and spiritual observances permeated the day-to-day activities as well as the annual and life cycles of Huron individuals. Jérôme Lalemant explained the difficulty this posed for the success of the Jesuits' mission in the early 1640s: "The greatest opposition that we meet in these countries ... consists in the fact that their remedies for diseases; their greatest amusements when in good health; their fishing, their hunting, and their tradings; the success of their crops, of their wars, and of their councils, – almost all abound in diabolical ceremonies. So that, as superstition has contaminated nearly all the actions of their lives, it would seem that to be a Christian, one must deprive himself not only of pastimes which elsewhere are wholly innocent, and of the dearest pleasures of life, but even of the most necessary things, and, in a word, die to the world at the very moment that one wishes to assume the life of a Christian" (23:53).

While all activities were characterized by religious observances and associations, the most important religious ceremonies, dances, and feasts were referred to as *onderha*, meaning the "prop" or "foundation" of the country (17:195–7). Within villages, Huron performed collective rituals and festivals, such as the midwinter soul-curing ritual of *Ononharoia*, for the good of the entire community. When Christian Huron refused to participate in rituals which the Jesuits had forbidden, they were accused by other Huron of trying to destroy their community. The Jesuits themselves were accused of trying to ruin the country by undermining the *onderha* (e.g., 26:279). Given the importance the Jesuits attached to Christianity as the source of moral, social, and political order, no doubt they would have expressed similar concern had they been in the position of the Huron. As in their dealings with the Montagnais, the Jesuits identified Huron shamans, known most commonly as *arendiwane*, as their rivals and sought to undermine their influence as much as possible.

When Huron traders arrived with their furs at Quebec in July 1633, the Jesuits tried to arrange for Fathers Brébeuf, Daniel, and Davost to return inland with them. Jean de Brébeuf had spent three years with the Huron before Quebec was taken by the English in 1629, and he was reasonably familiar with the language. Champlain encouraged the traders to take the priests by implying that they must do so in order to ensure the renewal of the French-Huron trading alliance (5:249–51). (The desire of many Huron to remain on good terms with the French for purposes of trade later proved to be a major factor in protecting the priests against those who accused them of witchcraft and argued for their death.) The negotiations were unsuccessful, and it was not until the next year that Brébeuf, Daniel, and Davost were transported upriver and eventually lodged in the Attignawantan village of Ihonatiria. The Huron then became the focus of the Jesuit missionary efforts in New France. What began with only a few priests grew, by 1648, to a total of eighteen priests and up to forty-six lay assistants (Trigger 1987, 665). These priests and assistants occupied the residence of Sainte-Marie, begun in 1639 and situated in the middle of the Huron country. Sainte-Marie was a fortified settlement that housed the Jesuits in European style and provided them with an independent subsistence base. It was also originally conceived as a base for the development of an exclusive village of Christian Huron (ibid., 665). This did not happen, however. The few Huron who resided within the settlement did so only for temporary visits or for refuge.

At the same time as the Jesuits' mission was growing, the situation of the Huron was becoming more and more precarious; the Iroquois, well supplied with firearms by Dutch traders, were engaging in increasingly intense warfare against these northern allies of the French. As early as 1642, the Huron had been subject to raiding in the vicinity of their villages by western members of the Iroquois confederacy for the purposes of securing furs and European trade goods (ibid., 661). This was in addition to the attacks that were frequently carried out against Huron traders travelling down river to trade at Quebec and Trois-Rivières. The Seneca were the Huron's closest Iroquois neighbours, and after 1646 they combined efforts with the Mohawk to launch a more concerted campaign against all members of the Huron confederacy. By 1650 the majority of Huron villages had been destroyed by the combined effects of this warfare and the accompanying food shortages and diseases. Many Huron were killed or taken captive; those who were not were forced to abandon their fields to seek refuge on Christian Island in

Georgian Bay, thereby sacrificing the crops that would have provided them with food for the winter.

The Jesuits also suffered in the Iroquois attacks. Father Antoine
Daniel was killed in 1648, before the collapse of the mission; he
was shot by arrow and gunfire during a raid on the village of
Teanaostaiaë, on the southeastern frontier of Huron country. The
following year, Fathers Jean de Brébeuf and Gabriel Lalemant were
tortured to death after the destruction of the village of Saint-Louis.
Several other Jesuits were killed in this period. Casualties among
the Huron were obviously far greater than among the Jesuits, but
these Jesuits' deaths are introduced here in anticipation of the
importance that is attributed to them in the *Relations*. When it was
clear that the Huron had no choice but to abandon all their villages,
the Jesuits burned the residence of Sainte-Marie and destroyed its
fields so that neither could be used by raiding parties, and they
took refuge with the Huron on Christian Island. After this winter,
during which many people died of starvation, the missionaries and
the majority of the surviving Christian Huron retreated to Quebec,
where the refugees were initially settled on the Ile d'Orléans. Other
Huron dispersed among their Iroquoian-speaking neighbours,
including the Neutral and the Erie, in the Great Lakes region
(Tooker [1964] 1991, viii; Heidenreich 1978, 387). Many who took
refuge with peoples to the south were killed or forced to disperse
again as a result of continued warfare. Others survived as captives
or as adopted members of the Iroquois (Trigger 1987, 840).

Although the Jesuits continued to minister to the Huron who
retreated to Quebec, these Huron refugees were not the subject of
the Jesuits' most concerted missionary efforts and received only
minimal attention in the *Relations*. The priests maintained their
missions among the Montagnais along the north shore of the
St Lawrence, but they increasingly looked farther west to missions
among more distant inhabitants of the Great Lakes, as well as south
to the members of the Iroquois confederacy itself. Missions among
the Iroquois became possible after the forceful military intervention
of the French government in the 1660s and the establishment of a
more permanent peace. Colonization in the St Lawrence region also
increased after mid-century, both as a result of this peace and
because of the increased efforts of the French government to promote it, and the clergy became more and more involved in minis-
tering to the European population of the colony (Codignola 1995,

209). The Jesuits' mission churches continued, of course, both within the St Lawrence region and farther afield. In their missionary travels, Jesuit fathers ranged to the shores of Hudson Bay, the western Great Lakes, and along the Mississippi River, from its source to its mouth. Although their effectiveness won them converts, these missions were difficult and frequently unrewarding, and the reports on them were not animated with the heroic tone and initial optimism that characterized the earlier *Relations*.

CHAPTER THREE

The Wilderness

To satisfy the waste and desolate land, and to make the ground put forth grass.
Job 38:27

Behold, I send you out as sheep in the midst of wolves.
Matthew 10:16

The Jesuits characterized the land they had come to in North America as a wilderness – a place that was barren, abandoned, and frequently hostile. Their writings reveal that these qualities of the wilderness were both physical and spiritual, and were manifest in both the land and its human inhabitants. Physically, the land was barren because much of it had never been cultivated, and the Jesuits ceaselessly promoted the processes of domestication that would render the landscape more familiar and mark it as the site of human agency. The Jesuits belonged to a religious tradition in which the wilderness was the site of those who were abandoned, rejected, or unknown to God. The wilderness within was sin and separation from God, while the wilderness without was the place unmarked by Christian civilization and consequently the proper domain of animals rather than humans. In describing Aboriginal people as the inhabitants of this landscape, the Jesuits evoked a condition of wildness, named savagery, that included being barren, sterile, and debased by association with the habitat of beasts. They described the souls of the Native inhabitants of the Northeast as untended, like the uncultivated landscape, and referred to their ways of life as sensual and brutish, marked by the absence of shame and of the knowledge of sin.

A LAND LAIN FALLOW

Paul Le Jeune had much to say about the land of New France. In his assessment of the four things that "make a Country desirable," he placed "good soil" first (9:135–7). While his concern for the agricultural potential of the soil reflects an awareness of the practical necessities of settlement, his comments also refer to a specifically European understanding of the land and human relationships with it. From Le Jeune's point of view, New France had lain "fallow since the birth of the world" (8:13). Because most of the land had not yet been the scene of either agriculture or animal husbandry, Le Jeune and others interpreted it as unused and barren. The transformation of uncultivated land into agricultural fields was important because it rendered the land both fruitful, as the priests emphasized, and more familiar. Le Jeune's support of agriculture was also based on his view of it as a re-enactment of the biblically ordained relationship between humans and their environment. He invoked the latter in a comparison between New France and the Garden of Eden in which he referred to Adam's initial responsibility, stated in Genesis (2:15), to till and keep the garden. "New France," he wrote, "will some day be a terrestrial Paradise if our Lord continues to bestow upon it his blessing, both material and spiritual. But meanwhile, its first inhabitants must do to it what Adam was commanded to do in that one which he lost by his own fault. God had placed him there to *fertilize it by his own work* and to preserve it by his vigilance, and not to stay there and do nothing" (9:191; emphasis added).

Although Le Jeune may have overemphasized the scope of the work required by Adam in the garden, there could be no question – in the Christian view of things – that after the Fall, humankind had been condemned to derive its sustenance from the earth through labour.[1] One of the first activities of Le Jeune and his fellow Jesuits when they arrived in 1632 had been to work the soil, and the priests repeatedly promoted agriculture as the necessary basis of the colony and the primary means of making the land habitable.[2] When Le Jeune approvingly wrote of "the exclusion of those who, having drained off the wealth that can be gathered in this country, left it without settlers and without cultivation, – not having, in all the years they enjoyed it, cleared a single arpent of land" (7:257), he was referring to the rescinding of the trading monopoly of the de Caëns. The de Caën company included both Catholic and Protestant principals, and Le Jeune's comment bears evidence of the Jesuits' disapproval of Protestant involvement in New France. However, like most traders – Catholic or Protestant – the de Caëns were interested in the wealth that could be acquired through the fur trade, rather than in promoting colonization. Agriculture, with its emphasis on the physical occupation of territory, was the primary feature of colonization and thus did not occupy the same place in the fur traders' vision as it did in the Jesuits' (Young 1995, 31).

The extensive forests of the Northeast had to be cleared before the soil could be tilled and planted; this was both a necessary first step and a symbolically significant transformation of the landscape. Shortly after his arrival on the St Lawrence, Le Jeune declared, "Everything depends upon clearing the land. But oh, my God! What labor there will be in clearing a forest encumbered with fallen trees, I might well say, since the deluge" (5:185). Le Jeune was not alone in thinking that clearing the forest would reduce the cold, eliminate insects, and improve the quality of the air, making the land more habitable and more suited to European occupation (5:183, 6:29; Jaenen 1985, 409). These views were derived from environmentalist theories – newly popular after the mid-sixteenth century but already familiar to the classical and medieval traditions – which held that populations were natural to and consequently compatible with specific geographies and climates (Rubiés 1993, 160).

Le Jeune's comment also points to an interpretation of the forest as a visible indication of the land's neglected state – a state, in effect, outside history. Eighteenth- and nineteenth-century philosophies elevated and even romanticized the idea of nature. The Jesuits, however, wrote at a time when the forest was still viewed as part of a hostile natural world into which God had sent humankind after expulsion from Eden (Bloch and Bloch 1980, 27; White 1972, 12). It is clear that the priests found the forest threatening – too large, too thick, too dark. Brébeuf complained of the difficulties he encountered in trying to make his way through the "obscurity and entanglement" of the woods (8:79); Le Jeune wrote of the "horrid depths of the woods" (12:237); and when Father Gabriel Druillettes left to spend the winter with a group of Algonkin in 1647, he was reported to have entered "into the land of Shades, so to speak, – that is to say, amid frightful mountains and forests, where the Sun never looks upon the earth, except by stealth" (32:259).

As the scene of a hostile and alien otherness, and as space that was overwhelmingly undomesticated, the forest was a wilderness. Although generally defined as a place where human agency, culture, or civilization is absent, both the parameters and the qualities of the wilderness as evoked by the Jesuits are culturally constructed. In the Judeo-Christian tradition, the wilderness included not only geographic places but moral and spiritual conditions, frequently in combination. The wilderness appears in the Old Testament as both the site and the state of sin; it is that which prevails when the blessing of the Lord is withdrawn, leaving both the person and place in a no man's land of cursedness (White 1972, 13). As a "void into which the soul is sent in its degradation," the wilderness was a condition from which one was rarely retrievable (ibid.). It was most frequently evoked as a desert, wasteland, or otherwise barren and desolate place – the physical characteristics of the site meta-phorically conveying the spiritual condition of its inhabitants.

The arid and semi-arid landscapes of the Old and New Testa-ments were not of course the landscapes of pre-industrial Europe, where the most commonly occurring and visible wilderness was the forest. However, although the forest was a place of abundant vegetative growth, it took its place with the desert and other more visibly barren places as a potential spiritual and moral wasteland. In addition, while the wilderness could occasionally be the site of spiritual realization and communion with God, the conflation of the physical and spiritual attributes of the site and its inhabitants continued to predominate in Christian thought and European intel-lectual traditions. Because of the Christian doctrine of redemption, however, both the site and the condition were less irrevocable than they had been for the Hebrews (ibid., 17). Physically, as well, portions of the wilderness could be transformed into an ordered, domesticated, and safe space. It was with these underlying associ-ations that the Jesuits who came to New France promoted the reduction of the forest and the transformation of the cleared land into agricultural fields that visibly bore the mark of human agency.

The Jesuits' association between the wilderness of North America and the condition of its inhabitants is implicit in their general use of *sauvage* to refer to the people around them. *Sauvage* has a number of meanings and associated moral qualities, including something "not cultivated, tamed, or domesticated," as well as a person who lived "away from society, beyond the pale of its laws, without fixed abode" (Dickason 1984, 63). Etymologically, *sauvage* is derived from the Latin word *silvaticus,* referring to "a forest inhabitant or man of the woods," a meaning that continued in the *homme sylvestre,* or wild man of the woods, of European folklore

(Berkhofer 1979, 13). Although *sauvage* could denote self-imposed isolation in the context of reflection or Christian hermitage, by the time the Jesuits were writing, the term referred to those who were considered "rude and fierce" and living without the refinements of Christian civilization (Dickason 1984, 63). Savagery signified a condition of absence and degeneration, in contrast to a condition of civilization; in this way the two terms defined opposing states that were nevertheless dependent on each other for meaning.

Le Jeune's first identification of Aboriginal people as *les sauvages* occurred in his description of his arrival in North America, at Tadoussac, on 18 June 1632. He wrote that the leaves, buds, flowers, and fruit appeared and ripened very quickly, adding: "J'entends les fruicts sauvages, car il n'y en a point d'autres" (5:21–3). He followed this by writing: "C'est icy que j'ay vue des Sauvages pour la première fois" (5:23). Le Jeune's movement from the use of *sauvage* as an adjective distinguishing wild from domesticated fruit, to a noun signifying the people he saw at Tadoussac was easily done. A similar condition of wildness – of something "not cultivated, tamed or domesticated" – is inferred in both his uses.[3] In their repeated use of *sauvage*, Le Jeune and other Jesuits not only drew on the common assumption that Aboriginal people were not civilized, but they metaphorically conflated the people's condition with the condition of the landscape. As the landscape was wild and uncultivated, marked by the absence of history and showing ample evidence of the consequences of the Fall, so were its inhabitants. The Jesuits described Native people as barren souls, as the "thorns" and weeds of an untended garden, and as the "rocks and stones" of the parched wilderness of biblical tradition (6:113; 26:213).

Portions of the wilderness could, as indicated, be brought within the pale of human agency. Similarly, people who occupied the state of degeneration signified by savagery could be recuperated into history by the Christian message, just as the axe, hoe, and seed transformed forests into fertile fields. In the *Relation* of 1634 Le Jeune wrote that the French in the vicinity of Quebec responded to the news of one of the first Native baptisms with "tears of joy and satisfaction, blessing God for accepting the first fruits of a land which has borne little else than thorns since the birth of centuries" (6:113). He and other Jesuits repeatedly expressed their work of preaching and the goals of conversion through an agricultural metaphor that conveyed a domesticating power to the Word of God and to their own activities in delivering its message. The Word, translated into Aboriginal languages and spoken by the Jesuits, was the seed that was to bear fruit after having been planted in the minds of Aboriginal people. In the context of the New World, this particular rhetorical figuration both reinforced the view of New World peoples as having been spiritually untended and, in effect, equated the Christianizing process with the domestication, and bringing to life, of the landscape. Of the mission, Le Jeune wrote that it was "necessary to clear, till, and sow, before harvesting" (5:191). The priests tried to cast into the souls of their missionary subjects "some little grain of Gospel seed," which would "ripen in its time, God willing" (7:269). It was by sowing this seed of the Gospel that the Jesuits hoped to reap a "harvest of souls" (10:9; 11:19).

This transformation confers potency and the privilege of agency on the Jesuits at the same time as it situates Native people as the passive recipients of the priests' creative power.[4] The Jesuits' missions among non-European peoples were not unusual in relying on an oral practice that emphasized preaching and teaching (O'Malley 1993, 92; see also Comaroff and Comaroff 1991, 216). Oral delivery and teaching of the Christian message was a central component of the Jesuits' ministry even in Europe, and as a technique it had played a significant role in the early history of Christianity. The emphasis on oral practice also involved a belief in the potency of the Word, undiminished through translation, that must be understood in relation to an ideology of the Word in which the spoken word was powerful, replete with both creative and destructive energy. Among the many connotations of the Word of God is its efficacy at achieving change in the universe (Ong 1967, 182–3). The Word, communicated directly to humankind, is laden with a life-transforming force, capable of commanding the faithful and calling the hearer into the universe of Christianity (Comaroff and Comaroff 1991, 214).[5] As it was preached by the Jesuits in the New World, the Word symbolized – in the multiple connotations of the transubstantiation of the body of Christ, which was itself initially the embodiment of the Word of God – the sustaining substance of received doctrine and the generative, penetrating properties of insemination. There was power in speaking it, and in the *Jesuit Relations* this was related to the power to give life.

The Jesuits' use of this domesticating idiom and their reliance on the symbolic potency of the Word illustrates how language is never merely instrumental. Metaphors are not just descriptive devices; they powerfully transfer meaning from one realm to another. In this way they can be included among the devices which Fabian identifies as "ideological operators," being those things that make it "possible for an issue (or a kind of experience, a certain constellation of values) to pass from one discourse into another" (1983a, 176). The agricultural, inseminating idiom used by the Jesuits was consistent with biblical usage of this same trope. Christ's parables of sowing, in which the word and teachings of the Gospel are equated with seeds that are sown in various conditions may be the most apparent source of the Jesuits' imagery. In the New World this idiom functioned as an ideological operator by characterizing the work and effect of the mission in a way that situated Aboriginal people in the realm of a previously untended and unmarked landscape – "an unknown world" (28:99), barren of spiritual knowledge and reclaimable only by an agency that was external to them.

It also placed them outside history. Indeed, in the *Jesuit Relations* the state of savagery is very much one of being detached from historical processes and events which the Jesuits assumed to be universal. The priests amplified this ahistoric state by representing Aboriginal customs as manifestations of eternal, unchanging practices. The Aboriginal people described in the *Relations* are largely the subjects, or a generalized subject, of verbs in a timeless present tense, since what they said or did was not characterized as a specific or isolated incident but was depicted "as an instance of a pregiven custom or trait" (Pratt 1986, 139). In only his second *Relation*, for example, Le Jeune declared that "the Savages have always been gluttons" (6:251). A few years later he asserted that the inhabitants of North America were characterized by customs that were "grown old, and authorized by the lapse of so many centuries" (13:79). The apparently unchanging nature of these customs made it possible for the Jesuits to both explain and predict the behaviour of Native people in a generalized way.

Situated as they were in the seventeenth century, the Jesuits wrote from within a yet unchallenged Judeo-Christian vision of time. They calculated the past and future according to time as revealed in the Scriptures and marked by specific mythical and historical events. Indeed, for many people in Europe, the encounter with North and South America was the culmination of the historical trajectory foretold in the Bible, for it enabled the Gospel to be preached to all peoples of the world in all tongues and so heralded the coming of the Apocalypse (Leddy Phelan 1970, 18).

This conception of time was replaced by the secular time of the natural sciences during the European Enlightenment. After the eighteenth century, the texts of colonialism distanced so-called primitive or premodern populations on a scale of evolutionary time in which the primitive was a temporal condition that belonged to an earlier stage of social evolution (Fabian 1983b, 17–18). Europe, which was modern, enlightened, and in possession of science and reason, became the principal motor and subject of history, while colonized populations were depicted as having no histories of their own and certainly no histories that mattered. In the *Jesuit Relations*, Aboriginal peoples are subordinated to a universal history, but in a more inclusive way; this was because the time of salvation required that the peoples of North America should be, like all other non-Christian peoples, "always already marked for salvation" even if they had previously been unaware of it (ibid., 26). The subjects of the Jesuits' descriptions could, in principle, always be redeemed, whereas the primitive object of nineteenth-century evolutionism was distanced, spatially and temporally, from the European observer as being neither ready for nor capable of civilization (ibid., 18; see also Prakash 1992, 356).

THE KINGDOM OF WILD BEASTS

The original etymological derivation of *sauvage* from Latin roots referring to the forest and forest dwellers had the most literal relevance in the Jesuits' use of it to refer to the Montagnais and other Algonkian-speaking peoples, who spent several months of the year pursuing a hunting economy in the woods. The Jesuits consistently associated residence in the woods with the acquisition of traits that were inappropriate for human beings. Le Jeune's description of the forest as "the Kingdom of Wild Beasts" (7:107) accurately reflected an understanding, common in Europe, of the forest as the "scene and matrix of all untamed life" and as a place to be feared (Bernheimer 1970, 20). Human beings who chose to occupy this realm were believed to inevitably share the way of life and wildness of its animal inhabitants, remaining human but not easily recognized as such (29:283). Jérôme Lalemant, for example, described "a roving band of Algonquins" as living "in the midst of the forests, leading a life externally more like that of beasts than that of other Men" (23:231). Similarly, Barthélemy Vimont wrote that those who lived in the woods were "men born and brought up in the forests like beasts" (27:143). Because the French, or at least the Jesuits, were uncomfortable in the forests and did not "lightly venture to entangle themselves" in the "dense woods" (21:63), the ability of many Aboriginal people to survive in an environment which the priests understood to be a wilderness earned them a grudging admiration at the same time as it placed them closer to beasts than to men. Where a Frenchman "would find only hindrance," a *sauvage* would "bound as lightly as a deer" (21:119) and would know "better the ways of these vast and dreadful forests than … the wild beasts, whose dwelling they are" (21:63).

Only after several years in New France did the priests suggest that the woods could serve as a site of Christian observances and that a kind of spiritual purity could be achieved by forest dwellers who had converted to Christianity and maintained its practice far away from the corrupt influences of civilization (31:223-5; 32:283). In the *Relation* for the years 1643 and 1644, Vimont assured his readers that the Montagnais Christians normally resident in the village of Sillery had dutifully maintained Christianity during their winter hunting: "I think that Heaven takes pleasure in seeing these good souls adore God in the midst of the woods, where the devil had so frequently been worshipped, and in hearing the names of Jesus and Mary reechoed by those vast solitudes, which formerly repeated nothing but horrible yells and cries" (25:163). Similarly, Lalemant described the combined worship of a group of men and women in the vicinity of Trois-Rivières, writing that "each one sang and prayed in his own language the praises of the great God, and Jesus Christ was adored in the very depth of Barbarism, – in the midst of the forests which were known, not long ago, only by fauns and satyrs, or, rather, by Demons and their imps" (31:221).

In their descriptions of Christian worship in the forest, the priests convey a sense of the power of the Word to penetrate and illuminate the depths of the woods and drive out evil, just as it could, they believed, penetrate, illuminate, and reform the depths of savagery in human beings. More importantly, this shift in their representation of savagery and its relationship with life in the forest speaks to the very real difficulty the Jesuits experienced in trying to replace hunting with agriculture, and it illustrates that for them, more than for the traders, administrators, or settlers in New France, savagery could not be constructed in a way that was ultimately unrecuperable. However much their descriptions of savagery took on the rigidity of generalizations, they could not betray their need to make their mission both necessary and possible. Accordingly, their representations reveal an ambiguity and include alterations in emphasis and judgment that are related to their experience.

To live primarily in the forest was to depend on hunting and fishing, and the priests' assessment of these economies returns us to the religious traditions informing their promotion of agriculture along the St Lawrence. It was Le Jeune's oft-stated view that people who practised a hunting economy did not know how to make the "best use" (6:149) of the land. He referred to hunting and the frequent movement it required as a "way of doing" that was "not praiseworthy" (6:259), suggesting that to live by hunting alone was an idle and wretched way of life (11:195). The Jesuits were not unfamiliar with hunting, but in their experience it was the privilege of those whose position in a hereditary aristocracy provided them with the resources and leisure to engage in it as a sport. The Jesuits represented Aboriginal people whose livelihood depended primarily on hunting as easy victims of disease, as constantly at risk of starvation (8:57), and incapable of hard work and diligence – "preferring to live in repose and in the idleness of animals" (11:143).

Biblically, hunting is opposed to agriculture and pastoralism as a lifestyle of those who are outside proper human community (White 1972, 16). White's (ibid.) exploration of the biblical genealogy of the medieval Wild Man myth reveals that "cursedness, or wildness, is identified with the wandering life of the hunter" and is opposed to the more stable life of either the shepherd or the farmer. In the Old Testament, the archetypal wild men "are the great rebels against the Lord, the God-challengers, the antiprophets, giants, nomads – men like Cain, Ham, and Ishmael," all of whom are represented as "wild men inhabiting a wild land, above all as hunters"(ibid., 14). While agriculture and pastoralism received varying degrees of favour at different places in the Old Testament, hunting and food gathering economies not only received little prominence but were symbolically superseded in the betrayal of the hunter Esau by his brother Jacob (Frye 1990, 142–3, 150–1). The metaphors of harvest, vintage, and the tending of flocks are particularly prominent in many of the central teachings and rituals of Christianity and were reinforced, even dependent upon, the experiences of agricultural and pastoral economies. Thus, in the hunting economies of northern North America, the priests were confronted with people whose way of life was not just, in their view, qualitatively unsuitable for Christianity, but for whom much of Christian language and ritual would have had little meaning.

While the Jesuits' preference for the Huron, who grew corn and lived in permanent villages, had a practical, logistical base, it must also be understood in the context of these attitudes toward hunting and agriculture. Brébeuf, for example, wrote of the Huron: "I do not claim here to put our Savages on a level with the Chinese, Japanese, and other Nations perfectly civilized; but only to put them above the condition of beasts, to which the opinion of some has reduced them, to give them rank among men, and to show that even among them there is some sort of Political and Civil life. It is, in my opinion, a great deal to say that they live assembled in Villages ... that they cultivate the fields, from which they obtain sufficient for their support during the year; and that they maintain peace and friendship with one another" (10:211). The Huron, to their credit, lived "in towns, not wandering about after the manner of wild animals, or even like many other savages" (11:7), and this stability in settled communities was favourably compared with wandering "like beasts through the forests" (34:21). These assumptions informed the priests' repeated argument that the project of converting non-sedentary Montagnais groups depended on settling them in permanent villages (6:147).

The negative connotations of non-sedentary economies are also implicit in the Jesuits' use of *vagabons* and *errans* to characterize those who practised them. The Latin base of the Old French *errer* and the English "to err" is *errare* – "to wander, hence to be deceived" (Partridge 1966, 186). In both the historical and contemporary usage of erring, physical wandering provides a metaphor for spiritual confusion and error. Dante's representation of himself as a lost and wandering Christian at the beginning of the *Divine Comedy*, waking to find himself "astray in a dark wood, confused by ways with the straight way at strife" (1965, 3) is one of the best literary illustrations of this. Dante's journey into hell began, notably, in a forest "wild and dense and dour" (ibid.), while his transition between purgatory and the journey into heaven occurred in something more like an Arcadian glen, where the path was strewn with flowers (Clark 1952, 1949). In Christian imagery, to live properly is to follow a straight and narrow path. Metaphorically, the pastoral wanderings of sheep alluded to in Psalm 23 and elsewhere are innocent only insofar as they are undertaken under the guidance of the shepherd, who prevents the flock from getting lost (cf. Frye 1990, 161). Otherwise, wandering, particularly through an uncharted wilderness, "inevitably leads one astray" (Taylor 1984, 11). It was in the context of this conceptual framework that Le Jeune asserted that when "the mind has strayed from the path of truth, it advances far into error" (6:217).

In reference to the unknown whereabouts of a potential neophyte, Le Jeune expressed his regret over the "misfortune" of the Montagnais, referring to them as "descended from Cain, or from some other wanderer like him" (11:269). While the priest's speculation about the origins of these New World peoples reinforced the negative associations of wandering, it also significantly assigned them a place within the Adamic lineage. This, as well as his assertion that "souls are all made from the same stock" (5:231), reflects an orthodox, monogenetic view of the origins of all humankind from one single act of creation, and firmly situates the peoples of North America within the "great family of the world" (7:167). To argue otherwise would risk departure from the book of Genesis and would result in potentially heretical positions (Hodgen 1964, 222). Other Jesuits alluded to homogeneous origins (4:117), as well as to an inevitable common destiny, in their arguments that Christ had shed his blood for the inhabitants of the New World as well as for anybody else, and that to doubt this would be to doubt God (14:165; 28:63).

However, while the *Relations* speak to the assumptions of Christian universalism and monogenesis that informed the Jesuits' mission, they also suggest that Aboriginal people flatly contradicted these assumptions. The Jesuits described how the latter asserted that their world and the world of the French had been the result of separate creations and that, because of this, the rules laid down by the God of the French were of no relevance to them (10:135; 11:9). In making this argument, the Aboriginal people pitted a relativist vision of time, space, and ideological relevance against the Jesuits' universalist vision, and by contesting it, resisted it. In this as in other instances, the authority and power of the truth claimed by the priests was deflected and decentred by the existing cultural logic of the people they were trying to convert to Christianity.

Le Jeune's comment on the wandering habits of the Montagnais is evocative of the theories of migration that were used to explain the physical location of the people of North and South America, so long unknown to Christendom. These theories were not new, having been developed in accordance with Scriptures to explain the peopling of the Old World, including Asia and Africa, as well as the presence of diversity in customs, manners, and religions. The postdiluvian dispersal of the sons of Noah was the one most frequently referred to for this purpose, although the breaches following the wanderings of Cain and his descendants mentioned by Le Jeune, as well as the confusion following the Tower of Babel, were similarly understood to have resulted in the spread of populations and the first divergences from an original, homogeneous tradition (Hodgen 1964, 230, 228).[6] As populations spread from the central hub of the Mediterranean, they found themselves farther and farther away from the original traditions and correct knowledge of God, and mistakenly replaced the knowledge they had lost with a variety of idolatries and false religions. In this view, the movement of populations only contributed to the degeneration that was thought to be the inevitable consequence of the Fall. Those who had moved farthest to the peripheries and away from the originary centre, as in the case of New World peoples, were more subject to degeneration than others. This emphasis on degeneration reflected a surviving medieval philosophy of history in which humankind and civilization were assumed to be in gradual decline, in a world whose life span was not only predetermined but was approaching its end (ibid., 262–4).

Remnants of the original tradition could, however, be discerned in the midst of what were otherwise errors. This was a common feature of missionary observations of New World religions. Indeed, the theory of migration and degeneration was very effective in enabling seemingly disparate histories and mythologies to be incorporated and realigned within a single trajectory of time and history. Le Jeune's conversations with Carigonan and an elder Montagnais during the winter of 1633 led him to conclude that "as to the Messou, they hold that he restored the world, which was destroyed in the flood; whence it appears that they have some tradition of that great universal deluge which happened in the time of Noë"(6:157). He added, however, that they had "burdened this truth with a great many irrelevant fables."[7] He repeated this interpretation a few years later, when he described a discussion he had had with another shaman who expressed some curiosity about Christian teachings. Explaining how the world had been repopulated by the sons of Noah after the flood, Le Jeune told the shaman "that their nation had sprung from this family; that the first ones who came to their country did not know how to read or write, and that was the reason their children had remained in ignorance; that they had indeed preserved the account of this deluge, but through a long succession of years they had enveloped this truth in a thousand fables; that we could not be mistaken about this event, having the same beliefs as our ancestors, since we see their books" (11:153).

In this passage, Le Jeune embraced the history of North America within a single, Christian vision of time and then defended his statement by calling on the superiority of writing as a means of preserving and recording the truth. I will return to the issue of writing, and its authority as a signifying practice, in chapter 5. Here, Le Jeune's comments are consistent with the prevailing belief that the absence of a system of alphabetical writing was a sign of the absence of history and of civilization (Mignolo 1992, 317–18). I have already shown how the Jesuits' descriptions of Aboriginal people living in a land that has been lost to time suggests that the latter have no history. Their references to the fallible and essentially fictive nature of oral tradition reinforces this denial of the separate history of Aboriginal people. It is as if the movement of history has happened everywhere but in the New World. The Jesuits' mission involved the initiation of this abandoned land and its inhabitants into the written record of the only history that mattered – the universal history of Christian salvation. Aboriginal people took their place in that history when they were baptized and had their names "written in the Book of life" (7:267; 9:33).[8]

THE STRENGTH OF BRUTES

The Jesuits frequently commented on the physical stature and appearance of the people they were trying to convert to Christianity. In doing so they conveyed an image of physically attractive and adept men and women whose bodily strength and endurance was superior to that of the average French person. When speaking of the "good things which are found among the savages," Le Jeune wrote, approvingly: "If we begin with physical advantages, I will say that they possess these in abundance. They are tall, erect, strong, well proportioned, agile; and there is nothing effeminate in their appearance. Those little Fops that are seen elsewhere are only caricatures of men, compared with our Savages" (6:229). Nevertheless, while the inhabitants of the New World may have been "well made men," their need to be physically proficient was indissolubly linked with the condition and category of savagery.

A useful comparison can be made with the Wild Man of the European tradition, for whom – it was believed – degeneration into a condition of wildness had resulted in the development, as compensation, of physical skills that were absent among those who lived within the pale of civilization (Bernheimer 1970, 9). In the *Relations*, the physical skills and endurance that derived from the condition of savagery could not compare with the advantages of Christian civilization; indeed, these skills were present because the latter were absent, and this absence spoke to the necessity of the Jesuits' mission. Thus, while the Jesuits knew that many Native people thought that they and other French were inferior in physical beauty and endurance, they tolerated this, secure in the belief that they had "a higher calling" (Jaenen 1974, 271; 5:239). Brébeuf characterized this difference by giving the following warning to prospective missionaries: "Leaving a highly civilized community, you fall into the hands of barbarous people who care but little for your Philosophy or your Theology. All the fine qualities which might make you loved and respected in France are like pearls trampled under the feet of swine, or rather of mules, which utterly despise you when they see that you are not as good pack animals as they are. If you could go naked, and carry the load of a horse upon your back, as they do, then you would be wise according to their doctrine, and would be recognized as a great man, otherwise not" (12:123).

Certainly, the Jesuits' life of study and teaching would not have equipped them well for physical exertion in any context, whether in Europe or North America. Although this was by no means a condition that all French men and women shared with the priests, the Jesuits did not compare Aboriginal people, physically, to peasants.[9] The superior strength which the Jesuits attributed to most of the people they encountered was a key component of savagery, not of rusticity; it was represented as a quality of brutes and savage men and women, and it superseded the physical condition of all

French. In Brébeuf's comments, it was also contrasted with the achievements of learning and the knowledge of God, which were the Jesuits' own particular qualifications and their source of authority. An opposition between the mind and the flesh underpins much of the Jesuits' representation of Aboriginal people and is an important element in their elaboration of the condition of savagery. Native people are consistently associated with the flesh, and it is assumed that without Christianity – characterized as "such high and new knowledge" (31:223) – they are also without knowledge of things abstract or strictly spiritual. In this respect they are not only the opposite of the Jesuits, who are associated with the intellect and pursuit of intense spirituality, but are subordinated to them.

The Jesuits used a spatial metaphor that opposed the flesh and the spirit hierarchically, as part of a set of hierarchies of "high and low," which applied to "the human body, psychic forms, geographical space and the social formation" (Stallybrass and White 1986, 2). That is why their own spiritual knowledge was so clearly referred to as "high" and worthy of respect, while the position, condition, and knowledge of Aboriginal people, who apparently paid more attention to their flesh, was naturalized as low. In the way this hierarchy was mapped onto the human frame, the spirit and achievements of the intellect were associated with the upper body, while the biological processes and physical desires that should be subordinate to the mind were associated with the lower body. Similarly, seventeenth-century moralists advanced theories of the passions that arranged the passions and reason – which they also thought of as will – in a dualistic hierarchy, as two parts of the soul. While the inferior passions moved the individual unthinkingly toward the satisfaction of appetites, reason and free will existed as superior parts of the soul and could be exercised to restrain these passions and direct the soul to God (Briggs 1989, 284–5).

Without the ability to command these passions, human beings would be no different from beasts and, significantly, would lose the opportunity of salvation. This view is apparent in the *Relations*, where Le Jeune and other Jesuits represented Native people's apparent concern for satisfying physical appetites as behaviour more appropriate to animals (who had nothing else to strive for) than human beings created in the image of God. It also provided the Jesuits with much of their sense of authority, though they had difficulty persuading Aboriginal people to recognize that authority.

In the *Relation* of 1634, Le Jeune portrayed a conversation between himself and the shaman Carigonan, which contrasted Carigonan's apparent fleshly degradation with the Jesuits' pursuit of higher things. Le Jeune described Carigonan as pointing to his flesh while stating, "Do not speak to me about the soul ... that is something that I give myself no anxiety about; it is this (showing his flesh) that I love, it is the body I cherish; as to the soul, I do not see it, let happen to it what will" (7:135). Le Jeune in reply called on Carigonan to exercise his will and restrain his physical appetites: "Hast thou any reason? ... Thou speakest like a brute, dogs love only their bodies; he who has made the Sun to shine upon thee, has he not prepared something better for thy soul than for the soul of a dog? If thou lovest only the body, thou wilt lose both thy body and thy soul. If a brute could talk, it would talk about nothing but its body and its flesh; hast thou nothing above the brute, which is made to serve thee? Dost thou love only flesh and blood? Thy soul, is it only the soul of a dog, that thou dost treat it with such contempt?" (7:135).

It is of course difficult to know what Carigonan actually said or what Le Jeune understood him to say; it is probable that the two men only minimally comprehended each other and that the exchange described by Le Jeune represents nothing more than the priest's views. At the same time, given the state of hostility that existed between Le Jeune and Carigonan, one wonders if the shaman deliberately provoked the priest by saying what he knew would be most disagreeable to him. In any case, the statement attributed to Carigonan is not representative of the complexity of Montagnais spiritual beliefs.[10] Le Jeune concluded this dialogue by describing Carigonan as a "poor wretch" who was "never able to raise his thoughts above earth" (7:135), thereby firmly situating the shaman at the bottom of the hierarchy between the flesh and the spirit, and within the debasement of savagery that subordinated Carigonan to Le Jeune. Carigonan's thoughts about Le Jeune were probably no more generous.

In the *Relations*, the ability to overcome physical desires is a condition of spiritual transcendence, while the unrepentant entertainment of physical appetites is a characteristic of animals, savagery, and those who deny God. The Jesuits told the people to whom they preached that "in order to honor God and to be happy in Heaven, they must abandon vice; live as men, and not as beasts;

think more of their souls, that are immortal, than of a body that will rot after death" (27:51). They evoked the "pure spirit" of Christ as one that "destroys nature, and causes grace to live," finding "its delight and its repose, not in plush and satin, but in a soul enriched with loving fear" (27:181). In speaking of a sermon delivered by Brébeuf to a group of Huron, Le Jeune implied that the latter, in contrast to this ideal, found "all their happiness" in "sensual pleasures" (13:51). After his winter with the Montagnais families in 1633–34, he had similarly declared that the "greatest satisfaction" the Montagnais "can have in their Paradise is in the stomach" (6:251). Instead of eating merely to live, as he did, Le Jeune described the Montagnais as living only to eat, being "slaves of the belly and of the table" (10:177). The priests' critique of hunting frequently included the complaint that people who engaged in this way of life found their highest enjoyment in nothing more than a plentiful supply of meat (Altherr 1983, 273). Flesh, it was written, was "the paradise of a man of flesh" (41:127).

Similarly, when Jérôme Lalemant described the degeneration of a Christian convert who had succumbed to temptation and become involved with a woman whom the Jesuits did not recognize as his legitimate wife, he wrote: "The bonds of the senses and the flesh are terrible" (31:269). As members of a religious order, the Jesuits were not unusual in the use of physical mortification and discipline in their attempt to overcome these bonds and deny even quotidian appetites. Ignatius Loyola had provided careful directions for exterior penances in the Spiritual Exercises, which outlined many of the spiritual principles of the order and were undertaken by Jesuit novices as a series of exercises. Exterior penances included the denial of food and sleep as well as the infliction of sensible bodily pain "by wearing haircloth or cords or iron chains next to the flesh, by scourging or wounding oneself, and by other kinds of austerity" (Fleming 1978, 54–6).[11]

Penances of this type were performed to atone for sins and to seek grace, and also "to overcome oneself, that is, to make sensuality obey reason and to bring ... lower inclinations into subjection to ... higher ones" (Tetlow 1987, 34). Many such mortifications were practised by the Jesuits in New France. Brébeuf wore a hairshirt and an iron-pointed belt (34:183) and was reported to have prayed for the martyrdom he eventually received when he was tortured to death. Father Charles Garnier, who was killed without torture, was said to have sought mortification night and day. He "always lay on the bare ground, and bore constantly upon his body some portion of that Cross which during life he held most dear, and on which it was his desire to die. Every time that he returned from his Mission rounds, he never failed to sharpen freshly the iron points of a girdle all covered with spur-rowels, which he wore next to his skin. In addition to this, he would very often use a discipline of wire, armed, besides, with sharpened points" (35:125).

What is most important to consider when analysing the Jesuits' responses to and representations of Aboriginal people is that many of the priests' comments suggest that these disciplines were especially necessary in North America. For example, shortly after taking up residence in the Huron village of Ihonatiria in 1634, Brébeuf expressed concern that there was "one thing ... which might give apprehension to a Son of the Society, to see himself in the midst of a brutal and sensual People, whose example might tarnish the luster of the most and the least delicate of all the virtues, unless especial care be taken – I mean Chastity" (10:111). Earlier, Le Jeune had warned prospective missionaries: "The altogether angelic chastity demanded by our constitutions is necessary here; one needs only to extend the hand to gather the apple of sin" (6:67).

These and other references to New France as "a country where shamelessness is classed as a virtue" (26:287) refer primarily to the attitudes toward sexuality and sexual relations which the priests encountered in their mission field. Although Aboriginal people at times used celibacy in pursuit of supernatural power, the priests' practice of lifelong abstinence for spiritual purposes and their resultant horror of sexuality had no immediate parallels in the cultures of the peoples they were trying to convert to Christianity. At the time when the Jesuits began their missions in Huron villages, premarital sexual relations between young Aboriginal men and women were common and acceptable, and – to the consternation of the Jesuits, as well as the Recollets who had preceded them – were initiated by either sex (Sagard [1939] 1968, 121–6). This was in considerable contrast to the sense of shame and sin associated with sexuality in Christianity and the rigorous control exercised over it by the church, including its enforcement as an act of procreation strictly within the context of the sacrament of marriage, where it was monitored in some detail through confession (Foucault 1980, 19).

The Jesuits quickly associated what they described as the shame-lessness of Aboriginal men and women – especially the fact that Aboriginal people did not consider the chastity of women more important than that of men – with the debasement of savagery and evidence of the influence of the devil. Brébeuf's statement also suggests, however, that because the priests found themselves in a situation that was uncircumscribed by a shared set of assumptions (including a sense of guilt and shame and the expectation of priestly abstinence), the suppression of desire and the negation of their own bodies required more effort and thus became more imperative. The ideological moorings that reinforced abstinence as a virtue rather than a purely cultural convention were less secure in the New World and hence required greater articulation.

The Jesuits' representation of this situation and their elaboration of the preciousness of purity consequently added emphasis to the distinction between themselves, as exemplars of impossible inno-cence, and Aboriginal people as the corrupt and possibly contami-nating other. After the death of Brébeuf, Ragueneau wrote: "His chastity was proof; and in that matter his eyes were so faithful to his heart, that they had no sight for the objects which might have soiled purity. His body was not rebellious to the spirit; and in the midst of impurity itself, which reigns, it seems, in this country, – he lived in an innocence as great as if he had sojourned in the midst of a desert inaccessible to that sin" (34:191–3). Ragueneau was, it seems, aware of the existence of the "objects which might have soiled purity," and Brébeuf's apparently unrebellious flesh may have been an ideal that many envied but could not so easily emulate. The priests' struggle against the flesh – their own impossible desire and their disgust at that desire – reinforced their frequent representation of Aboriginal people as the manifestation of the corruption they were afraid of and from which they had to dissociate themselves.

THE BLOOD OF THE MARTYRS

In summarizing the general sentiments of the missionaries, Le Jeune wrote: "The heart grows according as its works for Jesus Christ increase; and New France is the most suitable country in the world in which to understand the literal meaning of these beautiful words, *Sicut misit me vivens Pater, ita et ego mitto vos,* 'I send you, even as my Father has sent me.' *Ecce ego mitto vos sicut oves in medio*

luporum. 'Behold, I send you as sheep in the midst of wolves'"
(8:173). Le Jeune's use of the words of Christ to his apostles is
consistent with the Jesuits' view of their apostolic labours and their
frequent comparison of the incipient church in North America
and the primitive church of the first centuries of Christianity. A
frequent predator of the sheepfold and the bane of shepherds, the
wolf is figuratively used in the Bible to refer to the enemies of
Christians. Le Jeune's description of the Jesuit fathers as sheep in
the midst of wolves continues this image of a pioneering church
struggling against unbelievers and those who would destroy it –
"the fierce wolves who will come in among you, not sparing the
flock" (Acts 20:29).

As the mission continued, the Jesuits used the lupine metaphor
most frequently in connection with the Iroquois, especially as the
latter's incursions along the St Lawrence and into Huron country
became more deadly and more frequent. Like most peoples of the
Northeast, the Iroquois conducted a style of guerrilla warfare that
involved small-scale surprise attacks and was disconcertingly unfamiliar to most Europeans. The Jesuits never failed to remark on
this difference, describing Iroquoian raiding parties as "footpads"
who come by stealth and "besiege highways, never showing themselves except when they find their advantage" (22:249): one "would
almost as soon be besieged by Goblins as by the Iroquois; the latter
are hardly more visible than the former" (27:221). The French
population around Quebec was small and its military resources
limited; this situation, combined with the unfamiliarity of guerrilla
warfare, meant that the French were ineffectual and vulnerable
when faced with the Iroquois as an enemy. The fear and anxiety
accompanying this position is evident in Jesuit descriptions of
Iroquois aggression. Prisoners who were unfortunate enough to fall
into "'the clutches of those ferocious beasts'" (14:103) or "the
claws of those tigers" (14:101), could expect to be "burned and
eaten by those devouring wolves" (14:99).

The possibility of being burned and eaten was not just metaphor-
ical; it referred to the torture, killing, and ritual cannibalism of
captives that was historically practised by the Iroquoian and some
Algonkian peoples of northeastern North America. Although captives were often adopted into families to replace members who had
been killed in warfare, others were subjected to prolonged and
painful torture over the course of one or several nights, during

which they were kept sufficiently alive so that their deaths could take place at dawn in full sight of the sun. Jesuits frequently witnessed these events, and the practice was well known to readers of the *Relations*. Le Jeune gave a detailed description of the torture of an Iroquois prisoner at Tadoussac in his very first *Relation*, stating that no one should be "astonished at these acts of barbarism. Before the faith was received in Germany, Spain, or England, those nations were not more civilized" (5:33). In this way, he established a link between torture and pre-Christian behaviour as well as between Christianity and civilization. He also gave his readers dramatic evidence of just how much the Jesuits' Christian mission was needed (cf. Le Bras 1994, 35).

Yet torture was in common use throughout Europe at this time, and as a public spectacle it would not have been alien to the French who encountered it in North America. Although Le Jeune associated it with savagery, this association belies the fact that in Europe as well as North America torture was never simply an expression of a "lawless rage," such as would be associated with the absence of law and order; it was the result of premeditated and often carefully controlled technique – planned, regulated, and sanctioned (Foucault 1979, 33). Champlain objected to torture when it was undertaken in his presence, but he did so on the principle that it was a dishonourable way to treat captives of war and should properly be reserved for the worst criminals and heretics (Biggar [1922–36] 1971, 2:101–4). Brébeuf tried to argue against it on the basis of its cruelty but could not deny, when pressed, that in France people were also put to death by fire. He insisted, however, that the fire was "only for enormous crimes" and that those who were subjected to it were not made to linger (13:75). The torture enacted on captives of war also had its parallels in Christian belief and imagery, and in this as well it was not strictly shocking to the sensibilities of the Jesuits or other Europeans. In its content and form, the Jesuits found a literal enactment of the torments endured by condemned souls in hell, and torture appears in the *Relations* as a visible manifestation in this world of the consequences of the absence of belief and the abandonment of and by God (13:63; 18:31; 29:263).[12] As such it was well suited as a sign of savagery.

The ritual consumption of portions of the victim that often followed the final killing of a captive elicited more emphatic disgust and moral condemnation from the priests. Cannibalism had no

immediate parallel in Europe, and because it was an act that was
viewed with particular horror, it figured prominently in descriptions
of foreign lands and customs as a signifier of the worst kind of
savagery.[13] In colonial discourses on Africa, cannibalism formed a
conventional and accepted syndrome of savagery in combination
with nakedness and pagan beliefs (Hammand and Jablow 1970,
36). Whether it was real, as in northeastern North America, or
imagined, its presence helped justify the civilizing, Christianizing
enterprise. The Jesuits were unrestrained in their descriptions of
cannibalism as an "act of lawlessness" (13:79) and "inhumanity"
(17:75, 95) that was "entirely opposed to reason" (13:79). They
informed Huron who defended the practice that it was only "for
dogs and wolves to devour their quarry"; human beings, they said,
"should be humane, especially toward their fellow creatures"
(27:235). The Jesuits were surely aware that Protestants criticized
the Catholic Mass – in which the body and blood of Christ are
believed to be transubstantially consumed – as a perversion and a
manifestation of cannibalism. They did not acknowledge this, however, in the context of their representations of New World cannibalism. They were aware, however, of the potential ambiguity of
the Eucharist, and they reserved instruction in the full meaning of
this ritual for only the most promising Christian neophytes.

Cannibalism received its greatest elaboration in the context of
Iroquois aggression, where it was represented as the act of a ruthless
predator, a human animal that failed to distinguish the humanity
of its victims. Barthélemy Vimont evoked this image of cannibalism
as the ultimate abandonment of the distinction between humans
and animals when he described a war party eating recently killed
prisoners in the presence of the surviving captives. Vimont based
his description on the account of an Algonkin woman who had
been one of the captives but had escaped: "When the supper was
cooked, these wolves devoured their prey; one seized a thigh,
another a breast; some sucked the marrow from the bones; others
broke open the skulls, to extract the brains. In a word, they ate the
flesh of men with as much appetite as, and with more pleasure than,
hunters eat that of a Boar or of a Stag" (22:255). Here, the figurative use of the wolf transforms whatever cannibalism did occur in
this instance into more than a manifestation of what the Jesuits
considered to be the worst kind of savagery and inhumanity. Cannibalism becomes a literal sign of the figurative meaning of the wolf

as an enemy or predator of the church. The Jesuits created an especially successful and potent image in this constant interplay between the literal – in fact, an act whose meaning in the context of Iroquoian culture, warfare, and religion was to them unknown but which would not have signified in any case – and the figurative, based on a metaphor that had its precedents in biblical imagery. With "stomachs hungering after the flesh and blood of all these peoples who hear us" (26:19), the Iroquois figured prominently in the *Relations* as the "true tyrants and persecutors of this new Church" (25:193) and the "enemies of the salvation of these peoples" (25:97). While Satan himself was the "infernal wolf" (17:191), the Iroquois were "half Demons" (22:255).

The Jesuits' representations of torture and cannibalism in the context of warfare are the more vividly dramatic because they and other French were potential victims. In these descriptions can be read the foreshadowing of their possible martyrdom as well as their hope that the risks described would garner the necessary military assistance from France, which was then embroiled in the Thirty Years War. Many Jesuits thought that martyrdom was necessary in order to plant the faith in New France. In a continuation of the imagery of domestication and sowing, the "Blood of the Martyrs" was "the seed and germ of Christians" (34:227), not least because the Jesuits believed that their willingness to die would impress people with the truth of their teaching (15:121, 139; 29:45). The first Jesuit to serve such a purpose among the Huron was Antoine Daniel. Daniel was killed in 1648 when the Iroquois took the village of Teanoastaiaë, reportedly just as Daniel was finishing Mass. Fathers Jean de Brébeuf and Gabriel Lalemant followed, both being tortured to death after the destruction of the village of Saint-Louis in 1649. Before this, Father Isaac Jogues had been taken captive by the Mohawk and submitted to public torture, as Father Bressani was after him. Although both these priests eventually escaped, Jogues later participated in a peace embassy to a Mohawk village, but he was assassinated in 1646. Describing what was by all accounts a political killing, Lalemant wrote that Jogues had given up his life "as a burnt-offering, at the place where he had already begun his sacrifice" (31:137).

The torture and death of these Jesuits was described in considerable detail in the *Relations*, where it was depicted as a loving sacrifice that was heroic and the pinnacle of self-abnegation. Martyrdom was a favour from God, and it represented the culmination of a life spent in submission and humility; it was also the fullest expression of the imitation of Christ that informed Jesuit spirituality and practice (Harrod 1984, 183). Jesuits such as Le Jeune not only saw images of the Christian hell in the kinds of torture they would suffer if taken captive, but they saw scenes reminiscent of the passion and martyrdom of Christ (Ouellet 1993, 72). Given who they were and the beliefs that motivated them as Sons of the Cross, it is not surprising that the priests interpreted these deaths as martyrdoms, though whether or not the Jesuits who were killed actually did die for the faith, strictly speaking, is questionable.[14] Determining the reality of marytrdom involves the question of perspective as much as it involves an empirical demonstration of events; this is because martyrdom is always necessarily an interpretation of events based on a particular cultural and religious framework. This is so even when a universe of shared belief exists; in sixteenth- and seventeenth-century Europe, Protestants who died in religious conflicts were both martyrs and condemned heretics.

Martyrdom is also a potent site for the affirmation of belief, and accounts of it are almost always hagiographic (Kelley 1981, 119). By representing these deaths as martyrdoms, the Jesuits seized on what was most threatening, alien, and indeed probable, and, at least in the *Relations*, made it not only meaningful but the scene of their own victory. Death by torture and the possibility of being eaten by the enemy during the enactment of cultural practices which the Jesuits found both frightening and incomprehensible – and which they interpreted not as cultural practices but as the manifestation of savagery and lawlessness – was transformed into one of the most significant and triumphant acts in Christianity. Indeed, martyrdom makes a triumph out of what one's enemies may have reasonably considered their own victory. In this way, Vimont could present the events taking place in North America as the unfolding of a Christian drama between good and evil, where "'the rage of our enemies augments our merit, and their fires, our glory'" (25:41).

The appropriation of form and meaning occurred on all sides in this encounter, and while the *Relations* describe the death of Brébeuf and Lalemant as a scene of glory for the Jesuits, they suggest that they were also the scene of resistance and triumph – or at least revenge – for many of the Native people involved. Many of those who participated in the torture of these two fathers were Huron who had earlier been captured by the Iroquois and been adopted rather than killed (34:145). They were familiar with the Jesuits' Christian teaching and, as some have suggested, blamed the priests for the increasing weakness of the Huron confederacy (Trigger 1987, 764). They not only tortured Brébeuf and Lalemant but used aspects of Christian ritual in doing so, including pouring boiling water over the Jesuits' heads in a mockery of baptism and laying a string of red-hot hatchet blades, in reference to a rosary, around Brébeuf's neck (34:35, 145). Ragueneau described the Huron who were involved in this torture as infidels and former "enemies of the Faith" (34:145). Certainly, if they had rejected Christianity before being captured, they would have been no less disposed to approve of the Jesuits' teaching and their presence in Huron country at the time of Brébeuf's and Lalemant's death, when the Huron confederacy was visibly weakening and the remaining Huron were divided in opposition to and support of the priests.

REDEMPTION

The Jesuits' elaboration of the attributes of wildness and the condition of savagery should not be equated with a view of Aboriginal people as non-human – as literally being animals. Although the priests' descriptions metaphorically situated Native people in the domain of animals, doctrinally the Jesuits were bound to the position that the people they were trying to convert were "men first, last and always" (Hodgen 1964, 405). While this may have been a necessary orthodoxy, it was not a position that the Jesuits had difficulty with or attempted to dispute. Paul Ragueneau, for example, argued that although they "live in the woods, they are nonetheless men" (29:283). Even the Iroquois eventually became the subject of the Jesuits' mission. It is perhaps more significant for the purpose of current debates that while the Jesuits associated a certain physical condition with the state of savagery, neither they nor their contemporaries equated moral, intellectual, or social conditions with visible biological differences, nor did they imply or assume that the customs or behaviour they associated with savagery were biologically innate and immutable. In the seventeenth century, savagery was a qualitative condition to which anyone could be reduced and from which all should, in theory, be redeemable. It did not preclude either reason or intellect; indeed, the Jesuits offered frequent testimonials to the intelligence of the people they met and worked among (e.g., 5:211, 231; 8:233; 10:21, 235, 259; 14:97; 15:79, 123; 19:39; 26:125; 28:63).

This contrasts considerably with representations of savagery and primitiveness in the colonial discourses of the eighteenth and nineteenth centuries, when newly emergent ideas of progress were fused with the new sciences of evolutionary biology in the assertion that Europeans, and more specifically the northern European male, represented the pinnacle of physical and social evolution (Comaroff and Comaroff 1991, 99–108). Throughout the eighteenth century a scientifically grounded idea of race – the primary sign of which was skin colour – came to be used to support arguments for the relative inferiority or superiority of populations on the basis of nature rather than nurture. Physical morphologies were arraigned as evidence of natural and thus morally defensible inequalities between the races, and the white man's burden came to include both instruction and overrule.

Current efforts to deconstruct race emphasize the social and political constructedness of racial categories as well as the historical specificity of different racisms (Gilroy 1990, 264; Hall 1986, 23). Race has long been an adaptable concept, having been linked to nation, culture, class, and biology in differing ways and in differing combinations since at least the eighteenth century. It is notable, however, that early descriptions of the original inhabitants of North America rarely referred to race under any guise. Vaughan (1982, 927), for example, has argued that while there was significant prejudice against Native Americans in the English colonies in the sixteenth and seventeenth centuries, this did not initially include an understanding of Native people as biologically – or racially – separate and automatically inferior. Colour as a means of distinguishing Native people was not important until the mid-eighteenth century. That was when the view of a humanity divided and ranked according to race became increasingly prevalent, so that the identification of Aboriginal people according to the colour red coincided with the scientifically legitimated attribution of inferior or superior qualities to peoples according to physical morphologies (ibid., 918). In New France in the seventeenth century, the French initially tried to promote intermarriage between French men and Native women (5:211), and this in itself suggests the absence of categories of racial difference and the related concern over the preservation of biological purity that was so integral to later colonial regimes (Stoler 1991).[15]

The Jesuits' attitude toward the people they described as *sauvages* is more usefully compared with the belief attached to the myth of the European Wild Man and Wild Woman, who were believed to have reached the condition of wildness not by a gradual, evolutionary "ascent from the brute" but by a descent (Bernheimer 1970, 8). They were human beings who had lost the distinguishing characteristics of civilization and who could, occasionally, be reclaimed. The Jesuits wrote in the context of a Christian belief which allowed that "men might degenerate into an animal state in this world through sin," resulting, in effect, in a humanity "gone wild" (White 1976, 124). This degeneration occurred when the protective bounds of the church and Christian civilization were absent. Redemption from this condition was difficult but nevertheless possible. For the Jesuits in particular, the soul was, in theory, constant and was always reclaimable through God's grace. In North America the Jesuits foresaw and tried to enact a program of reclamation and redemption, their goal being to "bring back to God men" who in their view were "so unlike men" (10:109).

CHAPTER FOUR

Law and Order

All who have sinned without the law will also perish without the law,
and all who have sinned under the law will be judged by the law.

Romans 2:12

LAWLESSNESS

Shortly after arriving at Quebec in 1632, Paul Le Jeune reported an incident involving a Nipissing man who had been struck and wounded by a French boy.[1] It is not clear why the boy had hit this man – perhaps through fear, hostility, or a combination of the two. Le Jeune states only that the Nipissing had approached the boy out of interest while the latter was beating a drum, at which point the boy struck the man over the head severely enough to result in a bleeding wound (5:219). The man's companions demanded that gifts be given to them to atone for the offence, reportedly saying to the French interpreter, "'Behold, one of thy people has wounded one of ours; thou knowest our custom well; give us presents for this wound'" (5:221). Le Jeune wrote that the interpreter responded by saying, "Thou knowest our custom, when any one of our number has done wrong we punish him. This child has wounded one of your people; he shall be whipped at once in thy presence" (5:221). As the boy was brought forward to be beaten, however, the Nipissing who were present prevented the punishment from being carried out. Like many Native people in the Northeast at that time, the Nipissing did not use corporal punishment against children and were shocked at the prospect (14:37; Tooker [1964] 1991, 56–7). Neither procedure was followed and no further mention was made of the offence.

Le Jeune described the incident by writing: "As there is no government [cõme il n'y a point de police] among the Savages, if one among them kills or wounds another, he is, providing he can escape, released from all punishment by making a few presents to the friends of the deceased or the wounded one" (5:219–21). The priest based this statement on his assumption about the nature of savagery – a condition in which government was absent – and on the fact that he did not see anything resembling French legal and governing procedures among Aboriginal people. As well, he would have been aware of the views on Aboriginal social and political organization that had been publicly expressed by key figures in New France's recent history, including the Recollet fathers. The Jesuits had worked with the Recollets between 1625 and 1628, when the latter had been of the firm opinion that the often substantial payment of reparation for offences, including murder, could not be recognized as real law and should not be engaged in by the French.

Le Jeune would also have been familiar with Samuel de Champlain's accounts of his experiences in the Northeast, in which he frequently stated that the people with whom he dealt in eastern Canada had no law or justice, or any comparable mechanism for the preservation of social order. After spending the winter of 1615–16 in the Huron village of Cahiagué, Champlain complained that parents did not punish their children, who he felt were consequently ill behaved, and that they had no laws "nor anything approaching them ... inasmuch as there is with them no correction, punishment or censure of evil-doers except by way of revenge" (Biggar [1922–36] 1971, 3:142–3). The Jesuits expressed their concern at the risks they encountered from people who did not fear punishment for murdering or harming someone, and in this they evoked a situation in which the normal mechanisms of justice were absent and people acted without restraint (27:53; 33:155).

The Jesuits' understanding of law was associated with a notion of order and security which assumed that the proper functioning of society depended on the recognition of religiously and politically sanctioned authority and on the observance of each person's place in a social and political hierarchy, which culminated in the position of the king, who was authorized by God. The law was an institution of social order, and it provided the means of punishing deviations from that order, through fines, imprisonment, torture, and death. The legal system and the repressive mechanisms it was authorized to employ also supported the power of the monarch and the state and, in doing so, preserved the realm. Although the Jesuits eventually granted Aboriginal legal systems a legitimacy that

Champlain had not, both Champlain and the Jesuits understood punishment (both in this world and the next) to be less a mechanism of power than a legitimate and necessary deterrent against wrongdoing and an essential element in an effective legal and political system. It is not surprising that in North America they took the absence of corporal punishment as a sign of the absence of law and assumed that, without law, social order could at best be precarious.

Police, the term used by Le Jeune and translated into English as "government," had long been used in the context of royal legislation. It referred to the ordinances that were made by the king, confirmed through time, and understood to provide for the preservation of the kingdom (Kelley 1981, 189). *Police* was also one of the three bridles, along with justice and religion, first defined and discussed in the early sixteenth century by Claude de Seysell, prelate, diplomat, and royal counsellor. Seysell wrote in support of the ideal of Gallican unity, based on *un dieu, un roy, une foi, une loy,* and identified religion, justice, and *police* as the "treasures of the nation" – a trinity of forces whose maintenance would preserve the power of the monarchy and ensure social stability (ibid., 188). The bridles both constituted the king's ability to exercise power and, ideally, restrained his ability to abuse it; by preserving order in the will of the prince, they also – through the analogy of the king's body and the body politic – contributed to balance and harmony in the larger social order (Keohane 1980, 36–7). While "justice" referred more specifically to the courts and the legal profession, *police* seems to have embodied law, government, and order in relation to one another. Seysell's three bridles were reinvoked by Henry IV at the end of the sixteenth century. Henry IV's assumption of the French throne followed half a century of religious and civil discord, and the bridles were of obvious utility in his attempt to restore social order and assert the authority of his own rule.[2]

In content and practice, the seventeenth-century French legal system combined canon, civil, and customary laws and drew on both the Germanic and Roman legal traditions. Customary law included oral tradition and varied from region to region. By the seventeenth century the personal administration of the law by the monarch had become impossible and was delegated to the Parlement of Paris. The authority of the law, however, continued to derive exclusively from the king, whose authority, as noted above, was sanctioned by God. Ideally, it was the king's obligation to respect the laws of the kingdom and laws of God that "set standards of Christian justice and morality which it was his duty to enforce" (Shennan 1969, 15). However, the divisive wars of religion in the second half of the sixteenth century were accompanied by an increasing association between the power to make laws and expressions of the royal command, with the effect that the law more frequently represented the will of the sovereign – *car tel est notre plaisir* – in a literal sense (Foucault 1979, 47; Kelley 1981, 193–4). This increase in royal authority continued through the administration of Cardinal Richelieu and Louis XIII, whose objectives were to centralize power in the position of the monarch at the expense of feudal lords. It was accompanied by an elaboration of the justification of this authority by the principle of divine rule and by a corresponding proliferation in charges of *lèse-majesté* (Church 1975, 51).

It is the challenge to the king as the source of the law, and by extension the established relations of power between monarch and subject, that Foucault has shown to be at the root of any legal infraction during the *ancien regime* (1979, 47–8). Crime was a threat to order in the kingdom and theoretically an offence to all who abided by the law, but because the law represented the will of the sovereign, the resolution of crime was not strictly a matter of mediation or simple redress between the immediate victim and the person who had committed the injury. Punishment was neither strictly about justice nor a negative mechanism in the form of deterrence and prevention. The punishment of criminals marked and confirmed their guilt publicly and symbolically reasserted the power of the monarch. This was particularly the case in instances of public torture and execution, when the body of the condemned man or woman became a concentrated locus for the demonstration of the king's exclusive right to employ physical force (ibid., 49). While physical torture was not the most frequent means of punishment in France, when it did occur its performance demonstrated the power of the sovereign in relation to his subjects. As a juridico-political act, its function was not to "re-establish justice" but to reconstitute and reactivate the power of a "momentarily injured sovereignty" (ibid. 48–9).

This degree of coercive power had no parallel among the Aboriginal peoples of the Northeast in the seventeenth century. While the physical torture conducted on war captives outwardly appeared to be as violent and punitive as that enacted on an executioner's scaffold in Europe, it did not occur in a similar context of political authority related to penal oppression. The torture of war captives did not justify and reproduce political power by marking that power on the victim's body, as a public execution did in Europe. Champlain and the Jesuits both initially looked to Aboriginal leaders to punish or prohibit behaviour, as in France, but they found that the authority to do so did not exist in any form they could recognize (Biggar [1922–36] 1971, 3:159; Thwaites 1896–1901, 6:15). After participating in warfare with a party of Huron men, Champlain complained that they had no system of command and would not obey his orders when he attempted to take charge (Biggar [1922–36] 1971, 3:74–5). Throughout the *Relations*, the Jesuits frequently described Huron and Montagnais leaders as having little authority and being able only to influence people through persuasion. Notably, Barthélemy Vimont commented that the "captains" were "very poorly obeyed by their people, because they use no violence" (26:117–19).

The absence of punitive physical sanctions does not mean that people did not try to increase their personal authority or status in the pursuit of power or that they could not put pressure on others to make them comply. Morantz (1982, 482ff.), for example, has shown that anthropological assumptions about the absence of active self-promotion and personal ambition in what are considered to be near-egalitarian societies do not necessarily stand up to careful scrutiny. Brébeuf characterized what he saw of Huron leadership by noting, "These Captains do not govern their subjects by means of command and absolute power; they have no force at hand to compel them to their duty." But he also noted, "There are, however, some who know well how to secure obedience, especially when they have the affection of their subjects" (10:233). While Brébeuf is primarily referring to personal influence, Huron headmen could in fact use violence and the threat of violence as a sanction in cases of suspected sorcery or treason – both of which were punishable by death – though to do so required the general support of public opinion (Trigger 1987, 67–8).

In his first years in New France, Le Jeune commented on the pride and independence that resulted from the absence of government which he associated with an unbridled savage life. He wrote of the Montagnais, for example, that they were haughty, full of thoughts of themselves, and "imagine that they ought by right of birth, to enjoy the liberty of Wild ass colts, rendering no homage to any one whomsoever, except when they like. They have reproached me a hundred times because we fear our Captains, while they laugh at and make sport of theirs. All the authority of their chief is in his tongue's end; for he is powerful in so far as he is eloquent; and, even if he kills himself talking and haranguing, he will not be obeyed unless he pleases the Savages" (6:243).

The "wicked liberty of the Savages" (5:177) was a continual theme in the *Relations*. Lalemant explained that "the Savages" were "free and independent to the last degree," and that this, along with other customs and habits that were wholly alien to the French, made it difficult to understand or respect them (32:249). Le Jeune reported the surprise of his host during the winter of 1633–34 when he told him "that France was full of Captains, and that the King was the Captain of all the Captains" (7:189). This was an apt if somewhat general reflection of contemporary politics in France, where the competing interests and privileges of the nobility were becoming increasingly subordinated to those of the crown. While the authority of any French monarch would have had no counterpart in Huron and Montagnais systems of government, it is not insignificant that the *Relations* were written at a time when a strong and central governing authority was seen by many in France as the surest means of preserving the peace and stability of the realm and preventing a return to the disintegration, violence, and bloodshed of the previous century's religious and civil wars (Church 1972, 21).

The assumption that Aboriginal societies were, in effect, lawless, and the desire to exert control in the face of this apparent lawlessness had already made it impossible to resolve incidents involving French colonists and the Native peoples with whom they interacted in and around Quebec. Although the first two of these incidents occurred before 1632, when my analysis of the *Jesuit Relations* begins, they are worth reviewing here as an informative backdrop to the Jesuits' actions and to the attitudes toward law and order that are expressed in the *Relations*. The first case involved the murder of two Frenchmen in the fall of 1617. One of the murdered men, a locksmith, had quarrelled with and then violently assaulted a Montagnais man named Cherououny. The reasons for this quarrel are unspecified. When the locksmith left Quebec on a hunting trip,

Cherououny enlisted the aid of a companion to follow and kill both
him and, of necessity, his hunting partner. After the bodies of the
slain men were discovered, the French armed themselves, and the
Montagnais (who knew the identity of the murderers) withdrew
from the vicinity of Quebec (Biggar [1922–36] 1971, 188–9, 196).
When a leading headman approached the French with the offer of
reparation payments, the Recollets, who were the only missionaries
in the colony at that time, responded by demanding that the
malefactors be delivered up for questioning (ibid., 3:190). Cherououny decided to comply with this demand, but when he and his
retinue appeared in the French fort, the Recollets informed him
that French justice required execution in the case of murder (ibid.,
196). The Montagnais who were present agreed that the death
penalty could be exacted, but they urged the French to forgive the
fault (ibid., 197–8)

Most of the French living at the Quebec post were willing to
accept the reparation payments – the traders in particular were
anxious to restore good relations and were willing to do so in a
way acceptable to their Native trading partners. The Recollets,
however, regarded the payments as a simple act of barter and made
their well-known refusal on the principle that the blood of Christians could not be traded for the skins of animals (Sagard 1866,
56–7). That this decision was contrary to the wishes of the traders,
many of whom were Protestant, did not concern them and may
indeed have reinforced their decision. The Recollets did not accept
that the public could bear responsibility for the behaviour of an
individual, who alone should be considered guilty, and they argued,
mistakenly, that to accept the payments would only encourage
further murder and ill-treatment of French colonists by the Montagnais and others (ibid.). These priests would have viewed murder
as an offence against God as much as against the French state (such
as it was represented in New France), and they could not have
sanctioned its resolution by means which they considered basely
material and which did not recognize Christian principles and
Christian law. At the same time, the French residents of Quebec
did not feel secure enough to proceed with an execution, and it
was agreed among them that they could be reasonably satisfied
with the suspect's confession and willing exposure of his life, and
that these should be considered as a form of judicial atonement
and "honourable amends" (Biggar [1922–36] 1971, 3:199–200).

In France, "honourable amends" was the condemned person's public declaration of the crime, and it was performed before the doors of a church prior to public execution or torture (Foucault 1979, 43).

A general decision was taken to await the return of the ships and Champlain, who had been absent in France over the winter, before resolving the matter. But Champlain did not recognize reparation payments as legitimate any more than the Recollets did – a view he maintained for the rest of his life. He would not consider following Montagnais procedures both because he did not recognize them and because he was particularly concerned with establishing the authority of the French in the St Lawrence region. Champlain was not primarily a trader – his interests lay in building a more permanent colony, and in this respect he had more at stake in establishing a familiar order of things. However, he suspected that an execution would create a climate of distrust and hostility between the Montagnais and French, endangering the lives of the latter and undermining the fur trade (ibid., 213). It was, in fact, unlikely that the relatives of Cherououny would have accepted an execution according to the dictates of French legal procedure, however religiously or royally sanctioned. So Champlain eventually decided to let the matter pass – neither demanding Cherououny's execution nor accepting reparation payments. Although this retreat from the demand for the execution of the murderer was in accordance with the opinion of the majority of the traders, Champlain suspected that the Montagnais would interpret it as cowardice. Cherououny was provisionally pardoned and barred from Quebec, but the acrimonious relationship that ensued between him and Champlain strained relations between the French and Montagnais to such an extent that the trader Emery de Caën, after consulting the king in France during the winter of 1622, urged that the incident be resolved once and for all by the issue of a royal pardon (Trigger 1971, 97–8).

The French granted this pardon at a ceremony attended by a number of Montagnais and Algonkin, as well as some Huron men who had come down river to trade. The ceremony seems to have been pieced together for the occasion by Champlain and the traders in an effort to combine the authority of a royal pardon, as they understood it, with the public demonstration and distribution of gifts familiar to their Aboriginal allies and trading partners (Biggar

[1922–36] 1971, 5:105). In a symbolic gesture, the French threw a sword into the St Lawrence, explaining as they did so that the fault would be pardoned and forgotten in the same way as the sword disappeared beneath the waters (Sagard 1866, 226). The French also made speeches during the ceremony for the benefit of the pardoned man as well as the audience, in which they asserted that they did not take presents for the death of their people, and that in the event of any future murders they would "insist on the punishment by death of the authors of the wrong, holding them as [their] enemies, as well as any who might try to prevent the infliction of such punishment" (Biggar [1922–36] 1971, 106–7). Yet Champlain felt that the pardon would be seen as having been granted through "lack of courage" and because the French "did not dare" put the murderer to death, rather than through charitable forgiveness (ibid., 5:107). Champlain's belief that the pardon gave the Montagnais and other Native people a "very poor opinion" of the French because they "had not shown anger at the crime" (ibid.) was fairly accurate. It also suggests that the function of an execution was as much about asserting power and authority as it was about serving justice.

Although Champlain and the others hoped to impress their Native audience with their view of the seriousness of such a crime and its inevitable punishment, their assertion that the pardoned man had received his life from the French king would have meant little to those assembled, nor could the French repair the initial impression of weakness that had been conveyed through the lack of any definitive action after the murder. The ineffectiveness of the pardon was made clear to the Recollet Gabriel Sagard the following winter while he was living in a Huron village. Sagard reported with some chagrin that the Huron men who had witnessed the ceremony made a mockery of it. Rather than being impressed, they joked about the small penalty one would have to pay for killing a Frenchman (Sagard 1866, 226). Sagard could only write that in this they were mistaken and, with some accuracy, he predicted that pardons would not be granted so easily when the French had more power (ibid.).

Champlain could claim some vindication when Cherououny was murdered, along with a Frenchman, while on a peace embassy to the Iroquois in 1627. He wrote, without discriminating between the two men, that they equally deserved death for having previously taken the lives of others: "As far as the Reconciled was concerned, he fully deserved death for having murdered two of our men just as cruelly at Cape Tourmente; and the said Magnan, who was native of a place near Lisieux, had killed another man by beating him with a club, by which he got into trouble and was compelled to withdraw to New France. Thus does God sometimes punish men who, thinking to escape His justice by avoiding one path, are overtaken by it in another" (Biggar [1922–36] 1971, 5:229–31). Champlain's view that the justice of God had caught up with these men would have been shared by the Recollets and, if they had been present, the Jesuits; it was consistent with a belief in the universality of Christian principles, according to which the peoples of North America no less than any others would eventually be punished or rewarded according to their works. Thus, however much Champlain had been frustrated in his attempt to exercise justice and to gain mastery over this aspect of the encounter between French and Montagnais people in the St Lawrence region, he had no doubt that the murderer would ultimately be confronted with God's laws and justice.

The Jesuits drew upon a similar logic in their attempts to explain the Christian world view. In a conversation with a potential convert, Le Jeune argued that this final judgment made sense of what would otherwise be an arbitrary and frequently unjust world:

I brought forth many other arguments to make him recognize the great Prince; I explained that he was just, that he rewarded each one according to his works. "You yourselves love good people, you hate the wicked; you do good to your friends, you punish your enemies. God does the same, especially after death. Can you imagine that two men, dying the one very good, the other very abominable, can be equally happy in the other life? Here below no reward has been given to the good one, no punishment meted out to the wicked one, – indeed, the upright man has even been despised and the wicked one honored; would it be possible for that to pass without justice being done, without something resulting from it? If this confusion existed in the universe, it were better to be bad than good, and yet thou seest the contrary. Understand then that he who has made all things also measures the actions of men, and that he will deal with them according to their works." (11:159–61)

Champlain's statement reflects an assumption that the laws of a state should not only be applied to enforce the laws of God but that they themselves were instruments through which God's will could be made known. Champlain emphasized this point when outlining his understanding of the difference between French and Montagnais legal procedures. Instead of the public being responsible for making reparation for a crime, said Champlain, "Amongst us ... punishment was only inflicted upon the actual murderer, and, when we had nothing but suspicion to go upon, we exercised great patience, awaiting the time when our God, the Just Judge, who does not allow the wicked to prosper in their crime, should at last permit the guilty parties to be discovered by accepted proofs that could not be gainsaid" (Biggar [1922–36] 1971, 6:14).

Champlain's knowledge of the poor view that most Huron and Montagnais had taken of the French because of the way this murder had been handled encouraged him to take a harder line in imposing justice in two subsequent murder cases. But the outcome was no more satisfactory. The first of these murders occurred in the fall of 1627, when two men were killed while driving cattle back to Quebec from the pastures at Cape Tourmente. Both the Recollets and the Jesuits were in the colony at this time. The Recollets would have kept to their original position and supported Champlain's attempts on principle, and the Jesuits agreed with them. Champlain demanded that the man suspected of the killings be handed over, and he took three Montagnais hostage, including the suspected man's son, pending his delivery (ibid., 5:244). When the suspect was brought to Quebec the following spring, Champlain had him arrested and imprisoned to await trial (ibid., 5:262). However, the suspected man denied having committed the act, and reparation payments were not offered to the French.

Although this imprisonment was more than Champlain had accomplished in the previous murders, he ultimately had to abandon his position. Food supplies in and around Quebec were very low in the spring of 1628, and the supply ships that had been expected to bring relief did not arrive. After the autumn eel fishing, the Montagnais tried to force Champlain to release the prisoner by selling eels to the French at extremely inflated prices (ibid., 5:298; Trigger 1971, 99). Even though some French were compelled to give up their coats and other possessions for this food, Champlain would not release the prisoner (ibid., 5:298). The Montagnais then agreed among themselves to sell no food at all to the French until the prisoner was released (Trigger 1971, 99). Champlain intended to await the arrival of the ships before proceeding to trial and judgment of the suspected man. He appears to have particularly wanted to set an example of the French judicial process, in which, in his view, they "did not do anything except on good and lawful inquiry"; this example would stand in visible contrast to the methods of disorder and lawlessness he perceived around him (Biggar [1922–36] 1971, 6:6). But such a demonstration of justice depended on power and functioned as a demonstration of that power, and this is what Champlain did not have. The impression he in fact conveyed was one of arbitrary and unjust action in the imprisonment of a man who denied having committed a crime.

Supplies at the colony became so low that the French were forced to dig for roots, and Champlain, aware that judgment would again be postponed, was obliged to release the prisoner. He did this on the premise of demanding that the Montagnais comply with a number of conditions, including the recognition of Chomina, his only Montagnais supporter, as their principal leader (ibid., 6:11–13). Although the Montagnais involved agreed to these presumptuous demands, they clearly had no intention of carrying them out, even if they fully understood what was being asked of them. Champlain seems to have suspected this. In the end, he wrote that he was compelled to let the prisoner go because of the scarcity of supplies and the growing threat of hostilities (ibid., 6:25). Champlain was again frustrated at not being able to set the kind of example he had hoped for, and the murder remained unresolved. His comments suggest that he wanted to set an example of the moral virtues of French justice. However, his belief that the French were conveying an impression of weakness and his frustration at not being able to take any definitive action reveal that the purpose of such justice was as much about demonstrating power as about morality. I have already pointed out that public punishment in France not only demonstrated the power of the sovereign but also reconstituted it. The French at this time did not have that kind of power, so Champlain could hardly enact punishment as a means of reconstituting it. For their part, the Montagnais resented what they felt had been the cruel and unusual treatment of one of their people – whose health had become so poor that he had to be carried away after his release – and their opinion of the French was further eroded.

Champlain again resorted to imprisonment after his return to Quebec in the spring of 1633 when another Frenchman was murdered, this time by a Weskarini Algonkin man from the upper

Ottawa River. The Ottawa River was part of the route used by the
Huron on their way to trade with the French in the St Lawrence,
and it was the route along which the Jesuits would have to pass if
they wanted to reach Huron country. The Jesuits were now the
only missionaries in the colony, and Le Jeune featured the murder
in his first two *Relations*. The motive for the killing may have been
the resentment felt by many Montagnais and Algonkin over the
plans of the French to reassert their trading monopoly against
competing European traders, particularly the British, along the
St Lawrence (Trigger 1987, 478). The enforcement of the monopoly
meant that Native traders would be constrained in their attempts
to get the best possible price for their furs. Le Jeune's first reference
to the murder reflected a sense of vulnerability in the context of
the lawlessness of savagery, as well as the Jesuits' ideal of martyrdom: "This shows you how unsafe our lives are among these
Barbarians, but we find therein exceeding consolation, which
relieves us from all fear; it is that dying at the hands of these
Barbarians, whose salvation we come to seek, is in some degree
following the example of our good Master, who was put to death
by those to whom he came to bring life" (5:225).

Two Montagnais men who had previously quarrelled with the
killer revealed his identity to Champlain, and Champlain had him
arrested and imprisoned (5:223). At the same time, several hundred
Huron traders who were on their way to Quebec were encamped
in the Ottawa Valley, having come to exchange their furs with the
French for the first time since 1629, when the English had taken
the Quebec fort. Champlain was informed of their presence and
intentions by Louis Amantacha, a young Huron who had previously spent two years in France, where he had been baptized and
been taught by the Jesuits to read and write French (Trigger 1966,
58–9). After his return to North America in 1628, Amantacha
frequently assisted Champlain and the Jesuits in their dealings with
the Huron. In this case, he carefully informed Champlain of
another murder, that of the interpreter Etienne Brûlé. Brûlé had
remained in New France after the defeat of Quebec by the English,
to whom he had transferred his services. He was killed by a Huron
in 1633, on the suspicion that he was compromising their trading
alliance with the French by negotiating a trading agreement with
the Seneca, one of the five members of the Iroquois confederacy
(Trigger 1987, 475–6).

Although the Huron responsible for the decision to kill Brûlé were apparently already aware that he had been disowned by the French, other Huron were concerned that the incident would compromise the trading relationship and be met with reprisals. Le Jeune reported that Champlain had reassured Amantacha of Brûlé's status as a traitor and had said that because of this there would be no attempt to seek justice for his death (5:241).[3] This reassured most of the Huron traders who were waiting upriver, even though the Algonkin with whom they were encamped insisted that Champlain would surely imprison and seek the death of a Huron in retribution for Brûlé's murder, just as he was doing in the case of the Algonkin who was imprisoned in connection with the recently killed colonist (5:239-41). After these Huron men arrived at Quebec to trade, they held a council with Champlain, during which they agreed to take Fathers Brébeuf, Daniel, and Davost with them on their return trip, thereby assuring the beginning of the Jesuits' much-desired Huron mission. During this council they also requested the release of the prisoner (6:7), having been asked to do so by the Algonkin.

Champlain did not agree to the release of the prisoner, and the Huron at the council let the matter drop (6:7). Le Jeune and Brébeuf attended the council and supported Champlain's position. Le Jeune explained in his *Relation* of 1633 that "Sieur de Champlain sought earnestly to make the Hurons understand that it was not right to restore [the prisoner] to liberty; and that, having killed a Frenchman who had done him no harm, he deserved death" (6:7). The prisoner's kinspeople then sent word that unless he was released and pardoned, they would kill any Frenchman who attempted passage along the Ottawa River (6:7-9). The leader of the Kichesipirini Algonkin, who stood to gain the most by impeding direct trade between the French and Huron, delivered this news to the Huron traders himself. On being advised of this threat, the Huron who had agreed to embark with the three Jesuits withdrew their offer, realizing that if the priests were attacked while in their company they could, by defending them, become involved in unwanted hostilities with the Algonkin (6:11). Le Jeune linked this latest development to the absence of law and government which, if present, would have enabled the Algonkin to constrain the prisoner's relatives. He wrote: "It will be said that the Captain of the tribe of the murderer ought to have seized all those who had wicked designs against the French. It is true; but I have already remarked above that these Savages have no system of government, and that their Captain has no such authority" (6:15). Champlain used both threats and blandishments in an attempt to sway the relatives of the prisoner from their position, but was unsuccessful. Accordingly, the Jesuits were forced to postpone the beginning of their mission until the return of the Huron traders the following year.

In the subsequent *Relations*, there is no direct mention of the prisoner's fate. If he had been convicted of the murder and put to death, it is unlikely that the Jesuits would have failed to mention the fact, especially as such an act would have had serious repercussions for themselves and the other French. In the absence of any reports of further hostilities or fears of them, it is most probable that, once again, Champlain had to retreat from his position and release the prisoner.

ALL THINGS TO ALL MEN

Although Le Jeune regretted the delay in beginning the Jesuits' Huron mission, he would not at that time have considered resolving the murder by accepting reparation payments any more than Champlain would. Le Jeune affirmed that "the French will not accept presents as compensation for the murder of one of their countrymen" and suggested that the Hurons' awareness of this difference contributed to their initial unwillingness to take the priests with them into their villages: "They fear that their young men may do some reckless deed, for they would have to give up, alive or dead, anyone who might have committed murder, or else break with the French" (6:19). However, while Champlain remained adamant in the pursuit of his initial policies and the views that supported them, the Jesuits willingly and successfully involved themselves in reparation payments several years after the establishment of their Huron mission. Their mission policy in all parts of the world was already one of adaptation and relative flexibility, expressed within a broader assumption of the universal obligation of all peoples to become Christian. Le Jeune expressed this policy clearly in 1657 at the conclusion of a chapter, written for the *Relations* after his return to France, which spelled out his understanding of the differences between Aboriginal people and the French: "The world is full of variety and change, and one will never find unalterable permanence. If one were mounted on a tower high enough to survey at his ease all the Nations of the earth, he would find it very hard, amid such strange varieties and such a medley, to say who are wrong and who are right, who are fools and who are wise. Verily, God alone is constant; he alone is unchangeable; he alone varies not, and to him we must hold fast, to avoid change and inconstancy" (44:297).

The direction of Le Jeune's statement suggests that it may have been partially motivated by the need to defend the policy of accommodation from the Jesuits' critics, many of whom attacked Jesuit concessions to local practices – most specifically in matters of religious ritual – as something similar to calculated opportunism. In both India and China, where the Jesuits performed the Mass in the language and dress of the local elite, they were accused of sacrificing the integrity of Christianity and its observances in the pursuit of quick conversions (Healy 1958, 151; Duignan 1958, 727). The Italian Jesuit, Roberto de Nobili, for example, adopted the dress, language, and dietary and caste-purity laws of a Brahmin, and is said to have avoided denying Hindu beliefs while trying to demonstrate Christianity as a more perfect truth. Nobili was called before the Inquisition in 1615 but was eventually cleared of the charges brought against him. However, controversy over Jesuit activity in China continued throughout the seventeenth century. The Jesuits also used accommodation to good effect in the European countryside, where they had initially been so effective as missionaries; but in this context as well, their policy was subject to criticism by those who called for more rigorous – and, frequently, unattainable – standards of Christian piety and behaviour (Briggs 1989, 351).[4]

For our purposes, it is more significant that accommodation required a conscious inquiry into the language, customs, and manners of the people the Jesuits hoped to convert, the better to be able to adapt to their customs, to distinguish between those that were impediments to Christianity and those that could be left alone or modified, and to understand the "dispositions" of their missionary subjects (17:9). The link between this acquisition of knowledge and the overriding agenda of conversion is clearly revealed in Lalemant's comment to the effect that "a great step is gained when one has learned to know those with whom he has to deal; has penetrated their thoughts; has adapted himself to their language, their customs, and their manner of living; and when necessary, has been a Barbarian with them, in order to win them over to Jesus Christ" (23:207–9). Some years later, Lalemant observed that the Jesuits in the Huron mission had "a greater knowledge than ever of their language, of their customs, and of the means that must be taken to enter into their minds and hearts, and, by winning them over to ourselves, to gain them for Heaven" (28:65). He compared this situation favourably with the Jesuits' relative ignorance at the beginning of their mission. The Jesuits' approach combines a seemingly benign cultural relativism with a more calculating link between the pursuit of knowledge and power, or at least the power of persuasion (cf. Cohn 1985, 283).

The Jesuits' policy of inquiry into local customs and languages caused them to realize that procedures for the preservation of order and the redress of injury not only existed among the Huron but were in fact effective in resolving offences and preventing their recurrence. Thus, when Brébeuf wrote that the Huron at least lived in settled communities and thus did not wander about like beasts, he suggested that it was wrong to assume that they were wholly without laws and government:

Besides, if laws are like the governing wheel regulating Communities, – or to be more exact, are the soul of Commonwealths, – it seems to me that, in view of the perfect understanding that reigns among them, I am right in maintaining that they are not without laws. They punish murderers, thieves, traitors, and Sorcerers; and, in regard to murderers, although they do not preserve the severity of their ancestors towards them, nevertheless the little disorder there is among them in this respect makes me conclude that their procedure is scarcely less efficacious than is the punishment of death elsewhere; for the relatives of the deceased pursue not only him who has committed the murder, but address themselves to the whole Village, which must give satisfaction for it, and furnish, as soon as possible, for this purpose as many as sixty presents, the least of which must be of the value of a new Beaver robe. (10:215–17)

At the time Brébeuf made this observation, the payment of reparation by communities and allied groups in the case of murder and injury had replaced the stricter obligation of the victim's kin to avenge a murder through the death of the killer or a close relation (Trigger 1987, 60). The murderer's kin, village, or confederacy members paid compensation to the corresponding group of the victim in a formal ceremony, at the end of which the victim's relations in return offered gifts to express their forgiveness and satisfaction (ibid., 60–1). The groups responsible for these reparations were most often the matrilineal clan segments that defined an individual's immediate kin. Members of the group were encouraged to contribute whatever they could to the payments, and people took pride in donating as much as possible to the communal effort (28:51; 33:241). Lalemant's comment that "here the mere shame of having committed the crime is the offender's punishment" (28:63) alluded to the importance of shame as an element of legal sanction. To give away one's wealth freely and generously was a source of honour and was important in the accumulation of prestige (Heidenreich 1971, 225). However, to have benefited from someone else's wealth – as in the case of someone who had committed an offence requiring reparation – was a cause of shame and dishonour. Reparation payments were socially effective because they shamed the guilty party before his or her kinspeople and discouraged repeat offences by making the guilty person obligated to his or her relatives for their assistance. As well, it was obviously in the interest of those responsible for the actions of the members of their kin groups to bring pressure to bear on anyone who had committed a wrong in order to ensure that a repeat offence did not occur.

The amount of compensation paid was not always the same; it depended on the rank (13:15) and sex of the victim. The Jesuits did not fail to note that the compensation paid for the death of a woman was more than that paid for a man: "For a Huron killed by a Huron, they are generally content with thirty presents; for a woman, forty are demanded, – because, they say, women cannot so easily defend themselves; and, moreover, as it is they who people the country, their lives should be more valuable to the public, and their weakness should find a powerful protection in justice" (33:243–5). Although Brébeuf's comments suggest that unresolved injuries could lead to bloodshed (10:219, 225) if compensation was not provided, the reparation payments usually enabled Huron to settle injuries effectively and without violence (Trigger 1987, 60). Men and women who were suspected of witchcraft and treason were dealt with more severely, nearly always being put to death (10:233; 8:123; 33:219). Both witchcraft and treason were seen as fundamentally antisocial activities and as such were a more serious threat to social and community integrity than either murder or wilful injury.

While the Recollets had not been able to accept that the public could be responsible for a wrong committed by an individual, the Jesuits understood that reparation payments did work effectively as a legal and social sanction. The Jesuits' recognition of the symbolic as well as material significance of gifts also enabled them to move beyond the Recollets' initial interpretation of the payments as a crude bartering of a life for material goods. Brébeuf first commented on the symbolic function of reparation payments when he noted the importance of metaphor in Huron governing councils: "Metaphor is largely in use among these People; unless you accustom yourself to it, you will understand nothing in their councils, where they speak almost entirely in metaphors. They claim by this present to reunite all hearts and wills, and even entire villages, which have become estranged" (10:219). In other instances, the Jesuits remarked on the symbolic importance of gifts given in a political context, where presents supported the "voice" of those who spoke in councils and served as "contracts, and as public proofs, which are handed down to posterity, and attest what has been done in any matter" (33:133).

The priests' attention to the use of metaphor and gift giving in councils was not incidental. In keeping with their pursuit of knowledge about Aboriginal practices, the Jesuits paid keen attention to the procedures and speech styles used in these and other gatherings in the hope that they could use the public forum of a council to their advantage. As Le Jeune noted, "If we could make speeches as they do, and if we were present in their assemblies, I believe we could accomplish much there" (7:275). This was in fact the policy that the Jesuits adopted, requesting access to councils and trying to imitate Native speech styles, including the use of metaphor, circumlocution, and repetition, when presenting their Christian message. Brébeuf was especially adept at employing these techniques. He was so successful as an orator that he won the respect of the Huron – and, at times, the agreement of some headmen that they and their communities would convert to Christianity, though these agreements were not made on the basis of an understanding that Christianity would wholly supplant other religious practices (13:171; 15:117–19).

In emulating these speech styles, the Jesuits appropriated the discursive mechanisms associated with authority in Aboriginal cultures in the Northcast, where leaders cultivated and were expected to display considerable oratorical skills. The Jesuits did this in an attempt to represent themselves as people who were also worthy of being heard. This was a position the Jesuits were accustomed to in France, where they spoke with authority and could expect to be listened to on the basis of their position in a hierarchy of social estates; as clerics, they had the right to legitimate speech – the "right to power through speech" (Bourdieu 1977, 648) – and exercised it. In emulating the speech styles used in the councils, the Jesuits recognized that learning Native vocabularies and grammars was not enough, and they aimed for a more thoroughgoing competence in Aboriginal languages that would enable them to establish themselves as speakers who could "impose reception" (ibid., 647).[5]

Brébeuf's assessment of reparation payments as "scarcely less efficacious than the punishment of death elsewhere" was echoed several years later by Jérôme Lalemant, who wrote that it "seems more effectually to repress disorders than the personal punishment of criminals does in France" (28:51). Likewise, Paul Ragueneau offered the opinion that the Huron method of justice was "no doubt very efficacious for repressing evil" (33:235). Ragueneau made this comment when describing the Jesuits' involvement in the process of reparation payments after the murder of Jacques Douart, one of their *donnés*, in April 1648.[6] Douart was killed just outside the Jesuits' settlement at Saint-Marie at a time of growing division between the Huron who supported or at least tolerated the Jesuits and those who strongly disapproved of the priests' influence and wanted them out of Huron villages. The Jesuits' presence was fraught with contradictory implications; for some, particularly those who decided to become Christian, it meant increased prestige when dealing with the French, access to trade goods and protection from enemies. Others found the missionary presence more intrusive and were overtly hostile to both the message and the potential influence of the priests.

The men who were responsible for Douart's death had intended the murder to serve as a catalyst through which they could mobilize public opinion against the Jesuits and force them out of Huron country (Trigger 1987, 746); if the Jesuits left, that would bring an end to the trading alliance between the French and the Huron, as all Huron were aware. This had been made clear at the time of the renewal of the alliance in 1633, when Champlain had emphasized that, for the trade to continue, the Huron must keep the priests in their villages. Concern for the maintenance of this political and economic alliance with the French, who had not initially appeared to be a threat to the Huron, had already preserved the Jesuits during the epidemics that swept the Huron country before Douart's murder, even though the Jesuits were believed to be sorcerers primarily responsible for the diseases and their lives had been threatened. The few Huron who also were suspected of witchcraft in connection with the diseases had been put to death with impunity (15:53). At the time of Douart's murder, the Huron were increasingly vulnerable to Iroquois aggression and could least afford to lose the alliance with the French; at the same time, the weakening of the Huron confederacy intensified the resentment of some Huron toward the Jesuits.

A meeting of the confederacy council was convened immediately after Douart's murder. Although the anti-Jesuit faction urged that the priests be forbidden access to Huron villages and that they be required to leave Huron country along with any Huron Christians who refused to abandon Christianity, this faction did not prevail over those who were unwilling to sacrifice the alliance with the French, both for purposes of trade and as a source of protection in the growing conflict with the Iroquois (33:231–3). So rather than banishing the Jesuits, the council decided to offer them reparation. Since the priests were aware that the hostility toward them threatened the future of their mission as well as French trade with the Huron, they chose to proceed according to the "custom of the country," accepting that this would be a legitimate means of dealing with the offence as well as the most effective way of restoring good relations, avoiding further violence, and gaining symbolic advantage from the incident. The Christian Huron encouraged the Jesuits in this decision and helped them with the process of seeking redress. Ragueneau explained the Jesuits' compromise – so different from the reaction of Champlain and the Recollets to the previous murders – by stating: "It would be attempting the impossible, and even make matters still worse, instead of improving them, to try and proceed with Savages according to the method in which justice is administered in France, where he who is convicted of murder is put to death. Every country has its customs, which are in accordance with the diverse nature of each nation" (33:233–5).

The Jesuits were summoned from Sainte-Marie to the council to hear its decision, and Ragueneau wrote approvingly of the eloquence of the elder who addressed them (33:235). The priests were told to state the compensation they wished, and they accordingly presented the council with bundles of sticks representing the number of gifts they expected to receive. The Christian Huron had counselled the priests to make a large request in order to emphasize the importance of the affairs of Christianity, with the result that the Jesuits requested approximately one hundred gifts, each equal in value to ten beaver pelts. This was the largest reparation payment recorded among the Huron, and it suggests that the Jesuits hoped to convey the sense that there could indeed be nothing more important than the faith (Trigger 1987, 748). In the process of accepting the gifts, the Jesuits gave presents in return to reaffirm their alliance with the Huron and indicate that the offence had been forgiven. They took the opportunity to include among the gifts one that was intended "to complain of the calumnies that were circulated against the Faith, and against the Christians" (33:247). In this instance, the Jesuits inserted themselves into Huron cultural practices in a way that was recognizable and meaningful to the Huron involved and also was ultimately to the Jesuits' advantage. It was followed by a decrease in at least overt hostility toward the Jesuits and the Huron Christians.

THE LAW THAT IS NOT OF EARTH

The Jesuits' decision to resolve Douart's murder in accordance with Huron methods was not equivalent to an actual preference for these methods over the French procedures with which they were more familiar; nor, as I have already suggested, did it represent a tolerance disengaged from their overriding agenda of conversion. The priests' accommodation in the resolution of Douart's murder was an exception, made in the midst of a continuing disapproval of Aboriginal methods of justice – not on the basis of their general effectiveness, but on the basis of their incompatibility with Christianity. Lalemant stated the reasons for this disapproval in a letter he wrote to the Reverend Father Provincial of the Society of Jesus, in Paris, after he had spent seven years in the Huron mission. His comments reveal an association between the requirements of Christianity and the concepts of obedience and submission that informed seventeenth-century French social relations and legal and governing procedures. He began by candidly expressing his doubts about the suitability of the Huron for conversion to Christianity: "I could hardly believe that there is any place in the world more difficult to subject to the Laws of JESUS CHRIST. Not only because they have no knowledge of letters, no Historical monuments, and no idea of a Divinity who has created the world and who governs it; but, above all, because I do not believe that there is any people on earth freer than they, and less able to allow the subjection of their wills to any power whatever, – so much so that Fathers have no control over their children, or Captains over their subjects, or the Laws of the country over any of them, except in so far as each is pleased to submit to them" (28:49).

Lalemant followed this by saying that there was "no punishment ... inflicted on the guilty, and no criminal who is not sure that his life and property are in no danger," and he referred to having seen individuals glory in the crimes they had committed, including murder and the betrayal of the peace, because they feared no punishment (28:49). He went on to describe the public responsibility for the reparation for wrongdoing and complained that whatever its overall effectiveness, this method of justice was "nevertheless a very mild proceeding, which leaves individuals in such a spirit of liberty that they never submit to any Laws and obey no other impulse than that of their own will. This, without doubt, is a disposition quite contrary to the spirit of the Faith, which requires us to submit not only our wills, but our minds, our judgments, and all the sentiments of man to a power unknown to our senses, to a Law that is not of earth, and that is entirely opposed to the laws and sentiments of corrupt nature" (28:51).

The Recollets who preceded the Jesuits in New France had realized that the people they were trying to convert to Christianity did not share their own assumptions about the nature of religious and political authority, and that this difference would make the work of conversion particularly difficult (Le Clercq 1691, 514–15). It is clear that by the time Lalemant wrote his assessment of the difficulties facing the mission, the Jesuits had come to a similar conclusion; Lalemant's comments amplify the Jesuits' oft-stated concern over the apparent absence of authority and coercive leadership among Native peoples and directly link this with the issue of conversion. Huron and Montagnais social and political organizations provided neither the words nor the analogous conceptual material that were needed to invoke an appropriate sense of the power and absolute authority of the Judeo-Christian God and the necessity for obedience on pain of eternal punishment. The Jesuits struggled to find the terms to impart the power and majesty of a God (8:185) who must not only be loved but must be feared and obeyed, and they wrote of the impediment that the "wicked liberty of the Savages" posed to the necessary submission "to the yoke of the law of God" (5:177). The faith did "not agree well with pride" (31:261), and the pride stemming from the relative independence that Native people enjoyed in their social and political relations was, according to Vimont, their "greatest vice" (25:157). This situation was in considerable contrast to the Jesuits' experience in Asia and the Indian subcontinent, where cultural differences did not wholly preclude shared assumptions about authority and the role of punitive sanctions in preventing its violation.[7] The *Relations* reveal that the Jesuits became convinced that the people they were trying to convert would not fully understand Christianity until they understood obedience, both to God and to others who were in a position of authority. This in turn could not be achieved in the abstract but would require an understanding of obedience, authority, and punishment in this life.

Thus, although they engaged in reparation payments in 1648, the Jesuits supported the establishment of more punitive methods of law and order whenever possible, always in the hope of instilling the associated concepts of obedience and submission in place of the "disposition contrary to the spirit of the Faith." They had the most success at achieving the former in communities where Christian converts predominated in number or rank, or where political and economic conditions gave them an advantage. These elements prevailed in the Huron village of Ossossané just before the destruction of the Huron confederacy, when the community came to be known as the Believing Village. Christian converts were a distinct minority in Huron country until the very last years of the Jesuits' mission there, when the increasing vulnerability of the confederacy encouraged many Huron to align themselves more closely with the Jesuits and, by extension, with the French (Trigger 1987, 633).

By 1648, the majority of the inhabitants of Ossossané were Christian, and in an unprecedented step they agreed among themselves to appoint as principal headman the priest who was responsible for the mission in their village (34:217, 105). In this position, Father Chaumonot was charged with preventing the observance of any dance, feast, or other practice that was incompatible with the faith, and with making sure that the community conducted itself in accordance with Christian morals and principles. It was in this village that the first recorded use of corporal punishment in child rearing appeared (in 1648), when a Christian woman beat her four-year-old son (33:179). This was a radical departure from the methods of child rearing favoured by the Huron since at least the beginning of French interaction with them, and it was a sign of the growing influence of the Jesuits with at least some of those who were Christian. Huron parents had formerly reacted with horror to the Jesuits' and Recollets' suggestion that they use physical punishment on their children and could not be prevailed on to adopt such a practice. For the Huron, physical coercion and public humiliation of any individual, whether child or adult, was unacceptable and potentially devastating. Indeed, it was not unknown for children who had been treated severely by their parents to commit suicide as a result of the humiliation (14:37).[8] According to the *Relations*, the boy who was beaten received his punishment without complaint, even offering his blows to God, although whether this was the full nature of his understanding of the situation is questionable (33:179).

Prior to this, more dramatic public punishments, including imprisonment, had appeared in the small community of Sillery, near Quebec. Sillery was the result of Paul Le Jeune's persistent efforts to create a village where Christian converts could settle and adopt agriculture, thereby giving up the wandering way of life which the priests viewed so poorly. Le Jeune was able to begin the village in 1637 after funds had been donated by Noël Brulart de Sillery, Commander of the Order of Malta, the nobleman after whom the village was named. Le Jeune's discussion of the benefits of settlement interweave the adoption of Christianity and civilized habits with the greater control that could be exercised over people who stayed in one place. He wrote that it "would be a great blessing for their bodies, for their souls ... if those Tribes were stationary, and if they became docile to our direction, which they will do, I hope, in the course of time" (8:57).

Le Jeune was familiar with Jesuit reductions in Paraguay, where the Guarani had been gathered into communities that were largely governed by the Jesuits, and his encouragement of reductions in the Northeast reflect a similar objective (Jetten 1994, 31).[9] Spanish missionaries in the Philippines in the sixteenth century also had

worked to reorganize indigenous people into manageable adminis-
trative units (Rafael 1993, 88). The purpose in the Philippines, as
well as in Paraguay and the St Lawrence, was to create a bounded
site where the missionaries could physically circumscribe their audience so that the message of Christianity could be conveyed and
then enforced. The arrangement also gave the Jesuits the opportunity to establish their authority: settlement was linked to submission to the management of the priests, either directly or through
the authority of Native leaders, and this was a necessary element
in achieving conversions (12:169). Le Jeune revealed this, pointedly
if accidentally, when he wrote, "If once they can be made to settle
down, they are ours. I am mistaken, I meant to say they are Jesus
Christ's" (11:147).

The first residents of Sillery were two Montagnais families, both
of whom were among the small number of Montagnais who were
already Christian. They were soon joined by more Montagnais and
Algonkin, most of whom had not converted to Christianity; indeed,
the majority of the population of the village was never predomi-
nantly Christian. Many people were attracted to the idea of living
in a French-supported village because of the growing economic
hardship in the face of declining fur and game resources, and
because of the increasing threat of Iroquois raids (Beaulieu 1990,
133; Jetten 1994, 39). These uncertainties had particularly affected
many of the Montagnais in the vicinity of Quebec (Bailey 1969,
35). While living at Sillery made people less vulnerable to Iroquois
attack, French aid in the form of food, clothing, and housing was
tied to conversion. There were other material advantages linked to
conversion. The Company of One Hundred Associates gave the
Christian residents of Sillery the same trading privileges that it gave
French habitants (16:33). These inducements, however, were not
enough to generate a Christian majority; nor did the Jesuits ever
manage to have agriculture replace hunting as the primary mode of
subsistence in the village (Ronda 1979, 7). In this, as well as in the
presence of so many non-Christians, the boundaries of Sillery were
likely more porous than the Jesuits had originally envisioned.

Although the non-Christians were the majority at Sillery, the
Christians dominated positions of leadership and were supported
in this by the Jesuits and by the French governor at Quebec. The
Jesuits' objectives in establishing Sillery must be kept in mind when
one considers that they organized a form of election – itself

unprecedented – that resulted in the selection of the leaders (18:99–101). The *Relations* reported that the Christians expressed considerable zeal and a desire to adopt severe punishments, similar to those they had seen used by the French authorities in dealing with various criminal matters, to ensure that Christian morals were maintained in the village. This, too, was in keeping with the Jesuits' desire to make Sillery a model Christian village. This is when Le Jeune wrote: "The most zealous Christians met during this winter, unknown to us, in order to confer together upon the means of keeping themselves in the faith. One of them, in making an address, said that he thought more highly of prayers ... than of life, and that he would rather die than give them up; another said that he wished he might be punished and chastised in case he forfeited the word he had given to God; a third exclaimed that he who should fall into any error must be put into prison, and made to fast four days without eating or drinking" (20:143–5).

While I have already suggested that the sentiments Le Jeune attributed to these Christians may have been exaggerated, there is no doubt that punishment began to be used at Sillery; these punitive measures did not occur in isolated missions but in the most densely occupied areas of New France, where the Jesuits' accounts could have been contradicted by other European observers had they not been accurate. Although Le Jeune wrote that the Jesuits responded to this zeal by encouraging moderation, the *Relations* reported very approvingly on the forms of punishment that were subsequently enacted – finding in them just what was needed to enforce obedience and proper Christian behaviour – so much so that it is reasonable to believe that the Jesuits not only supported but encouraged them. It is also possible that the Jesuits saw more in them than those who enacted them; and less. Points of view are always partial, as are representations, even when the observer claims both scientific objectivity and the ability to produce a complete description (Clifford 1986, 18; Haraway 1988, 581). The Jesuits' emphasis on evidence of Christian humility and submission in the *Relations* and their understanding of Native people's understanding of the punishments that were performed at Sillery occurred from within such a situated point of view and is necessarily partial. This does not mean that the Jesuits were lying; but the material in the *Relations* was framed by the Jesuits' conscious and unconscious choices, as well as by everything they couldn't know.

The first use of penal confinement occurred in 1640, with a man who, "having fallen into a somewhat gross fault, for he became intoxicated," was sent to Quebec and put in prison at the request of his Christian relatives (20:149–51). The man was, notably, a shaman, and it is possible that the Christian leaders who supported and apparently directed his short imprisonment did not do so strictly because of the immorality of his drunkenness but as a means of intimidating him. After his release they reportedly warned him that his previous "threats" (which are unexplained) did not cause them fear and that if he did not abandon his former practices and become a Christian, they would renounce their kinship with him and do nothing to resolve his death if he was killed as a sorcerer. This in itself would have constituted a more powerful sanction than the threat of further imprisonment, and while Le Jeune reported that the man was chastened and humbled, it is questionable whether this was a result of his imprisonment or of the threat of abandonment by his kin, or indeed a combination of the two. In Le Jeune's point of view it was clearly the former, and he described the incident as "the first act of justice that the Savages have administered" (20:155). To this he added, revealingly: "Little by little, and with tact, they must be brought into submission" (20:155).

After this, several descriptions of the use of physical punishment at Sillery appeared in the *Relations*. The Jesuits' descriptions emphasize the positive effects of this punishment, both as a means of enforcing a rigorous moral code among the Christians and in demonstrating the moral rectitude of Christian life to the non-Christians (29:81). They also suggest that the Christians' new-found interest in punishment was vigorously opposed by the non-Christian majority. The non-Christians wished to retain the social and religious practices that were prohibited for Christians, including polygamy, and they still viewed punishment as anathema (22:83; 22:125). The Christians, however, had the support of the Jesuits – to whom they appear to have reported all irregularities – and of the governor (18:135, 193; Ronda 1979, 11). In 1642 they resolved to take a baptized woman, who had left her husband, to the prison at Quebec. The Jesuits had already made it a practice, before performing marriages at Sillery, to explain "the laws of marriage" in a way that emphasized "the importance of obeying the ordinance of God and of the Church, and the disgrace they incur by clashing

with the authority of Monsieur the Chevalier de Montmagny,
our Governor, who would not hesitate to have those severely punished
who should discard their wives in order to take others" (18:127).
Although these explanations appear to have been directed exclusively at men – not an unusual practice for the Jesuits – it was
women who were most often the recipients of the punishment that
was used to enforce monogamy and prevent separation (18:107;
22:119–21).

The Jesuits' criticism of the informal nature of leadership in
Aboriginal societies was paralleled by their criticism of women's
relative autonomy and lack of obedience to their husbands, and it
is clear from the *Relations* that while conversion required both men
and women to submit to God and to those who represented his
authority on earth, the Jesuits expected women to be the object of
yet another level of submission (Leacock 1980, 27–9; see also
Anderson 1991).[10] The Jesuits complained of the practice of polygamy among the Montagnais and Algonkin, and of the ease of
divorce and separation of married couples generally. In their view,
relations between Aboriginal men and women had to be replaced
with Christian models of permanent and exclusively monogamous
marriages, based on male authority and the corresponding obedience of women and children (Devens 1992, 25). Men who were
involved in a polygamous marriage and wished to convert were
required to give up their "extra" wives. This was achieved with
varying degrees of success, and the women who became superfluous
not surprisingly tried to re-establish their relationship with their
husbands. These attempts were easily represented as shameless
seduction and as an impediment to the Christianity of the men
involved (31:269).[11] Montagnais women in the vicinity of Quebec
and Sillery in particular were aware that monogamy would result
in economic hardship for them, and they resisted it for that reason
(Leacock 1980, 31; 12:165). Thus, men's and women's experiences
of the consequences of the Jesuits' teachings frequently differed.

The woman who was being taken to prison tried to break away
– obviously not convinced of the utility of penance – but was bound
and placed in a canoe by the Christians. At this point a handful of
non-Christian men, appalled by what they were witnessing, tried to
intervene to prevent the woman from being physically coerced any
further, offering to defend her with force if necessary (22:83). The
Christians were reported to have responded by asserting that there

was nothing they would not do or endure in order to secure obedience to God, and this resolution was said to have "silenced the Infidels" (22:83). The woman asked to be taken back to Sillery, promising to be obedient in the future, and this compromise was accepted. Barthélemy Vimont, who was then superior of the Quebec mission, wrote approvingly: "Such acts of justice cause no surprise in France, because it is usual there to proceed in that manner. But, among these peoples – where every one considers himself, from his birth, as free as the wild animals that roam their great forests – it is a marvel, or rather a miracle, to see a peremptory command obeyed, or any act of severity or justice performed ... The Infidels still have the same ideas; but the Christians are learning, more and more, the importance of exercising Justice" (22:83–5).

Public penance by groups of people who had become involved in some disorder, particularly drunkenness, was also a frequent occurrence. Although these actions were represented as self-motivated, the Jesuits' role in defining the scope and nature of the punishment is suggested in Lalemant's description of one such penance: "As the ... Captains have no regular Justice, or any authority to punish the failing of their people, – we are constrained to serve them as fathers and Judges, preventing disorders by certain punishments which they accept very willingly" (29:81). However, while the Jesuits were desirous of assuming the position of judge and father, their goal was to establish a more significant transformation in Aboriginal societies. This objective required that the ideas of obedience and submission be naturalized to the extent that the Aboriginal leaders themselves could give commands and threaten punishment, and not be rebuffed in doing so.

Jérôme Lalemant thought he saw some beginnings of this shift in consciousness around Quebec in 1648. At the same time as the priests at Sainte-Marie were dealing with the murder of Jacques Douart, the new governor at Quebec issued a public ordinance prohibiting drunkenness and the selling and buying of alcohol on penalty of punishment. This ordinance was issued with the agreement of the leaders at Sillery. It was announced orally at Sillery, first in French and then through a Native translator, and was attributed to both the governor and the Sillery leaders (33:51). Because of the role of these leaders, Lalemant emphasized the importance of the prohibition as a sign of changing attitudes toward governance. In his description of the event, he compared it with the liberty that had previously characterized the same people who were now beginning to issue orders; but he also suggested that the French still had little power to command Native people:

From the beginning of the world to the coming of the French, the Savages have never known what it was ... to forbid anything to their people, under any penalty, however slight. They are free people, each of whom considers himself of as much consequence as the others; and they submit to their chiefs only in so far as it pleases them. Nevertheless, the Captain delivered a powerful harangue; and, inasmuch as he well knew that the Savages would not recognize the prohibition enacted by a Frenchman, he repeated these words several times: "It is not only the Captain of the French who speaks to you but also such and such Captains," whose names he mentioned. "I also assure you with them that, if any one should be guilty of the prohibited offenses, we will give him up to the laws and the usages of the French."

For Lalemant, this was "the most important public act of jurisdiction" performed since his arrival "in this new World" (33:51–3). He contrasted it with the consequences of freedom, which, while pleasurable, could "degenerate into license, or rather into the liberty of Wild Asses," and so required regulation and subjection to "the rules emanating from eternal law" (33:53).

The Jesuits' intention in establishing Sillery and in otherwise attempting to implement French-style justice is clear. It is also clear that the Jesuits gained influence and the ability to exact some compliance with Christianity and the rules associated with it in relation to the erosion of Aboriginal political and economic autonomy. This was especially the case after the Huron confederacy was finally destroyed and the Huron were largely thrown upon the charity of the Jesuits. It is unlikely, however, that the Jesuits were successful in establishing an understanding of obedience similar to their own, or even one approaching what was necessary for people to understand the Christian message as the Jesuits wanted it understood. Sillery was never as successful or as harmonious a Christian village as Le Jeune had hoped, and by the mid-1660s it had been abandoned by all of its Montagnais and Algonkin inhabitants.

The few Christians who appeared willing to adopt the punitive measures described in the *Relations* are not representative of broader transformations in Aboriginal societies. Indeed, at Sillery these punitive measures were hotly contested by non-Christians. While the Jesuits' descriptions of the punishments carried out at Sillery suggest the willing submission of some Native converts and thus offer evidence of the degree to which the necessity of obedience and pain of punishment had been accepted, these depictions cannot reveal the complexity of Aboriginal people's understanding of these events and ideas. The majority of Aboriginal people who converted to Christianity did so with a distinctively relativistic outlook, incorporating the Jesuits' message into existing cultural frameworks and interpreting the Jesuits' teachings through these frameworks. Moreover, these cultural frameworks were never static or fixed collections of customs and traditions. Cultural meaning is not produced in isolation and does not change only in times of crisis; it is continually produced and interpreted in relation to varying historical circumstances. While meaning is subject to more or less innovation in the context of changing social, political, and economic conditions, and in relation to the interplay of power, coercion, and resistance, cultural innovation itself cannot occur without reference to an existing system of meaning. I suggest that this was the case even among those who apparently adopted the more punitive measures which the Jesuits commented on so favourably in the *Relations*.

It is important to distinguish between the rhetoric of the *Relations* and the constraints of meaning through which the Jesuits actually attempted to implement ideas of obedience and submission, as well as their own authority. The Jesuits' descriptions of their frustrations, such as those expressed by Lalemant in his letter to his superior, discussed above, are revealing of the difficulties they experienced in their efforts to convert people and to convey the appropriate sense of the subordination involved in becoming a proper Christian. These difficulties frequently turn on the issue of translation, and they speak to the negotiations over meaning which the Jesuits were required to enter into with Aboriginal peoples. Le Jeune had written, early on, that knowledge of Native languages was one of the most essential components of their mission (6:27–9); his purpose in spending the winter of 1633–34 with a Montagnais family had been to learn the language. Language was the key to the interior consciousness – the "minds and hearts" (28:65) – of Aboriginal people, and when spoken properly and in the manner associated with authority in indigenous cultures, it was an instrument of persuasion, command, and rebuttal (cf. Ouellet 1993, 74). Le Jeune explained that learning Native vernaculars was essential because any missionary "who knew the language perfectly, so that he could crush their reasons and promptly refute their absurdities, would be very powerful among them" (8:37). More particularly, the Jesuits initially looked for and expected to find equivalencies in Native languages that would enable them to convey their message, having faith in the power of the word to remain undiminished through translation. Father Le Mercier wrote, with respect to the Huron language: "We gather up all the words from the mouths of the Savages as so many precious stones, that we may use them afterwards to display before their eyes the beauty of our holy mysteries" (14:11). In this, the Jesuits were confident in their knowledge that there was only one unified and unifying Word, which was representative of the undivided power and authority of God and was the basis of their own authority over Aboriginal people.

This conceptualization posits a Native audience that is passive, to be acted upon with the power of the Word, rather than as active agents whose cultural logics had the power to decentre the authority of that Word and of the Jesuits. More importantly, the *Relations* suggest that these equivalencies in the language were not found. Shortly after arriving in North America, Le Jeune wrote that the language of the Montagnais was rich in some things but poor in others. Specifically, it was missing "all words for piety, devotion, virtue; all terms which are used to express the things of the other life; ... all words which refer to the regulation and government of a city, Province, or Empire; all that concerns justice, reward and punishment; ... all these things are never found either in the thoughts or upon the lips of the Savages" (7:21). Le Jeune explained: "As they have no true religion nor knowledge of the virtues, neither public authority nor government, neither Kingdom nor Republic, nor sciences, nor any of those things of which I have just spoken, consequently all the expressions, terms, words, and names which refer to that world of wealth and grandeur must necessarily be absent from their vocabulary" (7:21). Sixteen years after Le Jeune made these comments, and only a few years before recording the circumstances of the ordinance at Quebec in 1648, Jérôme Lalemant similarly stated that it seemed that "neither the Gospel nor holy Scripture had been composed" for the Huron. Lalemant's explanation revealed the extent to which the necessity of translation exposed the cultural specificities of the Christian message: "Not only do words fail them to express the sanctity of our mysteries, but even the parables and the more familiar discourses of Jesus Christ are inexplicable to them. They know not what is salt, leaven, stronghold, pearl, prison, mustard seed, casks of wine, lamp, candlestick, torch; they have no idea of Kingdoms, Kings, and their majesty; not even of shepherds, flocks and a sheepfold" (20:71).

These difficulties suggest the degree to which the Jesuits' attempts to convey their message through languages that spoke to separate specificities resulted in the displacement of much of the intent and content of the message (cf. Rafael 1993, 21). The Jesuits complained that they could not "find a name" to make Native people "understand God" (8:185) and that they had to resort to glosses such as "him who has made all" (7:123), "the great Captain of men, he who feeds all the world," and "he who lives on high" (8:185). These glosses were not improved on over the years, so that even among those who did convert to Christianity, what power was and what authority was remained highly mediated. The priests were also faced with people who not only had no word or comparable concept of sin but who denied having ever committed it (6:137; 13:199–203, 211), who were repelled by the threat of eternal punishment (12:77; 23:189), and who held the belief – fundamentally incompatible with the Christian logic of reward and punishment – that there would be no distinction in the afterlife between the "virtuous and the vicious" (8:121; 11:161). In these respects, the Jesuits were faced not only with the conceptual slippages precipitated by translation but also with direct challenges to the moral authority of Christianity. Indeed, in 1637 Le Jeune recorded one man's suggestion that a God who threw people into eternal flames simply could not be good (11:207). Responses such as these undermined the Jesuits by making them the purveyors of a doctrine that was difficult to respect and – as I shall discuss in greater detail in the next chapter – was potentially harmful.

Even when a universe of shared meaning already exists, attempts to construct new regimes of truth are subject to fissures, resistance, and appropriations of meaning that render complete success impossible (Kondo 1990, 77–8). The Jesuits were operating in the absence of any such shared meaning and were thus under constraints that made achieving a totalizing hegemony even more difficult. These constraints included the necessity of translation and the related necessity of layering their message over and through other cultures, whose members questioned the very principles of Christianity and, by extension, the authority of those who promulgated it. The Jesuits were required to negotiate and struggle over meaning. This exposed their message to the kinds of conceptual slippages and contradictions that prevented the seamless imposition of their authority – even when they achieved compliance – as well as the notions of humility and obedience that were central to the message they were trying to convey. Although the priests were intent on entering into and possessing the "minds and hearts" (28:65) of Native people with ideas of submission and obedience, these intentions were never completely realized. This was not only because the Jesuits' interlocutors did not share their universalizing assumptions – having no comparable understanding of the exclusivity of religious belief – but also because the Jesuits' attempts to spread the word of God through Aboriginal languages foundered on the inability of those languages to convey their totalizing vision. Even in the face of the punishment that some Christians appeared willing to adopt, it is unlikely that the Jesuits and even their most penitent converts shared a similar understanding of the scope of the authority of the "divine Majesty" (13:75).

CHAPTER FIVE

Conversion and Conquest

Why hast thou smitten us so that there is no healing for us?
Jeremiah 14:19

He delivers the afflicted by their affliction, and opens their ear by adversity.
Job 36:15

The Jesuits hoped to promote the obedience and submission that was a necessary attribute of Christian life by reconfiguring Aboriginal social and political relationships. Conversion itself, however, and the Jesuits' ability to gain compliance most frequently occurred after a process of chastisement and humiliation that had been brought about by disease or the consequences of warfare. The Jesuits described the misfortunes that were increasingly experienced by Native people during the 1630s and 1640s as afflictions and crosses, and they wrote that these afflictions had an especially beneficial effect in inducing conversion and generating the humility and obedience that were appropriate to Christian behaviour. Le Jeune, for example, wrote that affliction "opens the eyes of the understanding" (14:183). He and other Jesuits argued that suffering was necessary in order to reduce the pride and independence that kept people from recognizing the necessity of submission and their obligations to God and the Jesuits. This understanding was pointedly expressed in the *Relation* for the years 1642 and 1643, which stated: "Humiliations are the harbingers that mark the dwellings of the great God; and tribulation attracts us more strongly and with much more certainty than does comfort. It is necessary to abase the pride and the haughtiness of these people, in order to give admission to the faith" (25:39).

THE HAND THAT SMITES THEM

Shortly after the Jesuits arrived in Huron country, many of the villages were stricken with a disease of European origin. This was the first of a series of epidemics that further reduced the Huron population by almost half over a period of six years (Trigger 1987, 499). Although the Jesuits and other French also became ill during the initial epidemic, they recovered and remained relatively unaffected as the outbreaks of disease recurred. This was in sharp contrast to the inability of large numbers of Huron to withstand the diseases, and it suggested to many of them that the French had some effective means of prevention and cure. The Jesuits were accordingly asked to help stop the sickness – at which point, they took the opportunity to insist that all Huron pray and believe in God, presenting this as "the true and only means of turning away this scourge of heaven" (13:159). While many people were initially prepared to adopt the Jesuits' terms, most did not realize the exclusive nature of the priests' demands, and they continued to seek other remedies, leaving the Jesuits to accuse them of hypocrisy and backsliding (13:165, 177).

As the diseases continued unabated, the Jesuits' proposed cures were soon discredited, though most Huron continued to believe that the priests had the power to protect themselves from the illnesses – a belief that was reinforced when the Huron observed the Jesuits spending so much time with the sick yet remaining "full of life and health" (19:93). For the Huron, withholding assistance from someone who was ill violated community reciprocity, and as a sign of disregard for the welfare of others it could only be motivated by hostile intentions. Such behaviour was easily interpreted as a sign of complicity in a disease that had been caused by witchcraft, which was believed to be the most common cause of incurable illnesses and the most frequent expression of antisocial, hostile sentiments (Trigger 1987, 66–7). Although the residents of most Huron villages first sought to identify and eliminate possible witches among themselves, the majority came to the conclusion that the French, and particularly the Jesuits, were causing the diseases through sorcery.

This interpretation of the Jesuits as witches was encouraged by the priests' reputation as successful and potentially powerful supernatural practitioners. Evidence that the Jesuits possessed power had already been apparent in their success in praying for rain and their ability to predict lunar eclipses (15:139, 175), as well as by a number of the technologies they had brought from Europe. Brébeuf had been involved in a successful bid for rain during his first years with the Huron, before the English defeat of the French and the removal of the missionaries to France (10:43–9). This was not forgotten by those Huron who knew Brébeuf, and during the very dry spring and summer of 1635 they asked the Jesuits to pray for an end to the drought. The efforts of Huron *arendiwane* to do the same had been unsuccessful. One shaman in particular blamed the Jesuits for his failure and demanded, much to the chagrin of the priests, that they take down the cross they had erected in front of their cabin in Ihonatiria (10:37–43). The Jesuits not only refused to remove the cross but they twice enjoyed seeing their prayers and processions followed by a significant amount of rain, as well as by the admiration and respect of many people.

Suspicion about the Jesuits' involvement in the diseases also stemmed from the fact that most Huron did not completely understand the priests' intentions in wanting to live among them (17:125). While it was accepted that traders and warriors had occasion to live with allies or trading partners, the missionaries' evangelical purpose, based as it was on a universalist belief, had no precedent and consequently was open to local interpretation (Trigger 1987, 534). As the diseases spread, the Jesuits' teaching and habits were easily shaped into indisputable proof of hostile intentions and sinister activities, whose ultimate objective was the destruction of the Huron people.

This was particularly the case with behaviour that was culturally alien and either oddly inappropriate or more directly suggestive of the stinginess and uncooperative spirit which the Huron associated with witchcraft. The priests' habit of closing their door at certain times of the day for private meditation, for example, fell within the range of antisocial behaviour, and many Huron believed that the Jesuits needed this privacy in order to practice their sorcery (15:33). Their practice of speaking to those who were sick about death and the afterlife was similarly unusual and inappropriate (15:23, 69). Most people found the priests' continual references to death disturbing and morbid, and they suspected that the Jesuits were concerned not with an individual's recovery but solely with sending him or her to heaven. The Jesuits attempted to aid the sick as much as possible, hoping to advance the cause of Christianity by discrediting the cures offered by the shamans and setting an example of Christian charity (15:69). However, at the same time as they were diligently attempting to bring people some relief, their stern criticism of Native curing rites and their refusal to participate in them were viewed by most Huron as socially uncooperative behaviour and interpreted as further evidence that the priests actually wanted to prevent people from recovering. In this way, although the priests cast their behaviour in the benevolent idiom of Christian charity and sacrifice, the Huron interpreted it through the divergent idiom of harmful intent and sorcery. Some Huron even suggested that the Jesuits' wish to see them in heaven as soon as possible caused them to shorten the lives of those whom they felt were best prepared for the afterlife (19:241).

The unfamiliar material and technological features of the mission were similarly subject to interpretation by the Huron, who saw in them further evidence of the Jesuits' sorcery. The act of writing, especially, was subject to a variety of appropriations that challenged the Jesuits' own understanding and their expectation of its significance. Writing was the Jesuits' most potent technology, both as the source of their universal truths and because Native people admired their ability to communicate silently through pieces of marked paper. The Jesuits based much of their faith in the truth of Christianity and its universal relevance on the authority of their written tradition. In their attempt to persuade people to convert, they lost no opportunity to assert the value of the Bible as a written document containing the authentic and undistorted Word of God. They argued that while oral traditions were subject to the fallibility of memory and the accumulation of lies and stories invented for the sake of entertainment, the basis of their own faith in the Word, not just spoken but recorded, was indisputable (11:153; 17:135). Le Jeune quickly identified the word used by the Montagnais to speak of the distant past, *nitatohokan*, as meaning "I relate a fable, I am telling an old story invented for amusement" (6:157). By comparison, when some Huron asked Brébeuf how the Jesuits "knew there was a Hell, and whence we obtained all that we told about the condition of the damned," he replied "that we had indubitable proofs of it, that we possessed it through divine revelation; that the Holy Ghost himself had dictated these truths to certain persons, and to our Ancestors, who had left them to us in writing, and that we still carefully preserved the books containing them" (13:51–3).[1]

The Jesuits' faith in the Bible as a written document was deeply embedded in an assumption that all truth and knowledge was textually dependent (Mignolo 1992, 318). The proof of God himself could be "read" in nature. As one of the priests explained, "The reality of a God was ... so clear that it was only necessary to open the eyes to see it written in large characters upon the faces of all creatures" (13:173). I have already noted that the Jesuits' mission in New France depended, in large part, on an oral practice and that the early history of Christianity was itself strongly oral, relying on an oral praxis of preaching and teaching the Word. However, the Jesuits came to North America after the Renaissance, when an ideology of the letter had emerged which emphasized the primacy of writing as well as the physical form of the book itself, both as the essential repository of knowledge and as its principal means of transmission (Mignolo 1992, 311, 318). While Christ himself was originally the Word of God embodied (11:169), the authority of this Word came to be the authority of the Book. Indeed, in an especially interesting gloss on Christ's physical embodiment of textual authority, Le Jeune referred to Christ as "the living Book" (16:123). Writing, knowledge, and the material form of the book convened in an ideology and philosophy of writing that had considerable effect on interpretations of the New World and its peoples; the absence of a system of alphabetical writing quickly came to be interpreted as a sign of the absence of civilization and as evidence of the inferiority of New World peoples (Mignolo 1992, 317–18).

The priests knew that "the art of inscribing upon paper matters that are beyond sight" (15:121) visibly impressed the people they were trying to convert. Notes sent between Jesuits from one village to another caused the Native people to think that the priests could predict the future and read minds at a distance, something that only shamans could similarly claim to do (Axtell 1988, 93). In 1635 Brébeuf wrote that the Huron admired the lodestone, prism, and joiner's tools, "but above all ... writing, for they could not conceive how, what one of us, being in the village, had said to them, and put down at the same time in writing, another, who meanwhile was in a house far away, could say readily on seeing the writing. I believe they have made a hundred trials of it" (8:113). He added: "This serves to gain their affections, and to render them more docile when we introduce the admirable and incomprehensible mysteries of our Faith; for the belief they have in our intelligence and capacity causes them to accept without reply what we say to them" (8:113).

However, while the technology of writing contributed to the aura of power and prestige which the Jesuits' were trying to cultivate, they could not control the whole meaning of the relationship between writing and power in the minds of Huron who suspected them of witchcraft. This relationship was quite different from the priests' understanding of the power of writing as a privileged vehicle of knowledge and the permanent repository and record of the Word of God. While it constituted proof that the Jesuits were figures of some unusual skills and power, it was precisely this power that would have enabled the Jesuits to harm people by causing inexplicable diseases through sorcery. That the Jesuits represented themselves as men who had come to North America only for the good of the Huron was irrelevant, since the Huron believed that powerful individuals did not use their power for good or evil exclusively but could put it to use for both purposes.

Thus, although writing initially contributed to the respect with which the priests were treated, as fears of the Jesuits' sorcery grew it also came to be suspected as a means by which the Jesuits targeted people for illness or otherwise spread the contagion. Lalemant explained in 1639 that if the fathers "asked the name of some one, in order to write it in the register of our baptized ones, and not lose memory of it, it was (they said) that we might pierce him secretly, and afterward, tearing out this written name, cause the death, by this same act, of him or her who bore that name" (19:129). Similarly, when Fathers Antoine Daniel and Simon Le Moyne visited the eastern Arendarhonon villages, some inhabitants of the principal village of Contarea claimed to have seen these fathers in dreams, "unfolding certain books, whence issued sparks of fire which spread everywhere, and no doubt caused this pestilential disease" (20:33). Dreams were not random occurrences for the Huron; they were prophetic of events, as well as of the innermost desires of the soul, and the Huron paid close attention to them (Sioui 1994, 297). In these instances, the symbolic significance of writing and its associated technologies slipped their moorings in the Jesuits' ideology and received altered significance at the hands of the Huron. Accusations that linked writing to witchcraft subverted the Jesuits' position as benefactors concerned with saving people rather than destroying them. In this way, they displaced the equivalence which the Jesuits were trying to convey between themselves and health and life. These accusations also denied the ideology of the letter that informed the priests' reliance on the book. By contesting the authority of writing, Aboriginal people acknowledged its power but denied its hegemonic function as the embodiment of a universal truth; in this way, if only temporarily, they refused the translation of colonial signifying practices and the authority embedded in them.[2]

In other instances, the ritual and pictorial symbolism of Christianity was appropriated and resisted in ways the Jesuits could neither control nor possibly have predicted. Many Huron had initially interpreted and received baptism as a healing rite; but as the diseases intensified, the Jesuits' sacrament of life came to be viewed as one of the ways in which they perpetrated their witchcraft. Many people refused it on the grounds that it was certain to kill them or their children. Others incorporated a facsimile of baptism into their own healing rituals, to the great annoyance of the Jesuits. This particular innovation first occurred in 1637, when it was introduced by a shaman who had fasted for ten days in an attempt to acquire insight into the cause and cure of the prevailing disease, and it involved sprinkling water on the sick (13:237–43). It appeared again in 1639, after a Huron man had a vision of Iouskeha, a central Huron deity, in which Iouskeha blamed the Jesuits for the disease and prescribed a healing ritual that involved drinking ritually prepared water from a kettle (20:27–9). The Jesuits roundly condemned the vision as the work of demons who were trying to defend their territory against the Jesuits, and they described the practitioners of the prescribed healing rite as "masqueraders" and "physicians from hell" (20:31).

The Jesuits' vigorous condemnation of these acts suggests the degree to which they frustrated their objectives. These acts also show the ambivalence of Huron resistance. The Huron did not wholly reject the content of the Jesuits' practices or the authority linked to them, nor did their actions leave Huron and French cultural meanings and systems of signification intact, within imaginary boundaries, with their contents unimplicated in each other (Bhabba 1994, 110). The Huron men and women who participated in these rites engaged the potential power of baptism as a healing ritual. In doing so, they allowed some of its significance while disallowing the Jesuits' monopoly over the meaning and potentially life-saving effects of the ritual and its water (20:29–31).

This time of illness and death was, understandably, fraught with the search for signs of the cause of disease. The life-size paintings of Christ and the Virgin Mary displayed by the Jesuits in their chapel in Ossossané were believed to possess magical qualities and to be two of the instruments through which the priests were causing illness among Huron who were unfortunate enough to have looked at the pictures (15:19). Paintings of hell, detailing the torments of the damned – intended to inspire fear and to encourage people to convert – were interpreted as literal representations of the sufferings of those whom the Jesuits had afflicted with disease. Le Mercier explained that "on the day of the baptism of Pierre Tsiouendaen-taha," the Jesuits "exhibited an excellent representation of the judgment, where the damned are depicted, – some with serpents and dragons tearing out their entrails, and the greater part with some kind of instrument of their punishment" (14:103). While "many obtained some benefit from this spectacle," some "per-suaded themselves that this multitude of men, desperate, and heaped one upon the other, were all those we had caused to die during this Winter; that these flames represented the heats of the pestilential fever, and these dragons and serpents, the venomous beasts that we made use of in order to poison them" (14:103).

In this instance, the Jesuits' teaching about heaven, hell, and punishment was deflected and was returned to the Jesuits with new and contrary meanings. Even the communion wafers became sus-pect. As a general principle, the priests had been careful to reveal the doctrine of transubstantiation (whereby the wafers became the body of Christ) only to the few Christian Huron whom they felt most trustworthy in the faith (15:33). In spite of this precaution, the host soon featured in a rumour suggesting that the Jesuits were causing the diseases through a corpse they had brought from France and were hiding in their residence (15:33).

Several years later, after the diseases had largely run their course, stories began to circulate among the Huron of dreams and visions through which people had learned that the Jesuits' teachings were not only wrong but were dangerous. In one story, the soul of a recently deceased woman returned, after having journeyed to heaven, to warn the Huron that all who had become Christian were being tortured in heaven as prisoners of war, by the French, just as war captives were tortured by the Huron and their enemies (30:29). This warning was especially subversive because it situated the Jesuits as enemies whose objective in making converts was to take prison-ers, rather than as people who had come to give the secret of eternal life. It also completely overturned the division between heaven and hell, which many Native people found especially problematic. These incidents demonstrate the decentring that can occur when signs that are supposed to stand for the authority of the colonizers – or, in this case, the missionaries – are exposed to interpretation and appropriation by the colonized; they also illustrate competition for control over the interpretation of events and for what passes as the truth. As assertions of Native beliefs that make sense of Christian symbolism and Christian figures in the context of these beliefs, they are also an ideological response in kind to the Jesuits.

However much the Jesuits were required to argue over meaning with the Huron while they were in the Huron villages, their own understanding of the cause of the diseases was forcibly and categorically expressed in the pages of the *Relations*. It revolved around the influence of the devil in inspiring the persecution against them (19:91) and the biblically precedented interpretation of disease as divinely instigated punishment and trial. After the initial accusation of witchcraft in 1636, Le Jeune wrote that the growing hostility toward the Jesuits was a positive sign that the demons – hitherto unchallenged as the masters of the country – had been "powerfully attacked, since they put themselves vigorously on the defensive" (11:41). A few years later, Father Le Mercier characterized the accusations and general hostility as part of "the war that the powers of darkness have openly declared against us" (14:109). The Jesuits described their work with the sick and their unflagging attempts to teach and baptize people in the midst of threats as a literal struggle against the forces of evil (17:191; 20:51). In view of the Jesuits' own understanding of their mission, the allegation that it was they who were manipulating supernatural powers for harm could only be understood and represented as a fundamental misinterpretation of their activities and proof of the blindness of their accusers. Jérôme Lalemant responded to the accusations brought against the Jesuits with righteous indignation, writing that the words of their accusers were "often only blasphemies against God and our mysteries, and insults against us, accompanied with incredible evidences of ingratitude, – hurling at us the reproach that it is our visits and our remedies which cause them to sicken and die, and that our sojourn here is the sole cause of all their troubles" (17:15).

The Jesuits soon came to represent the diseases as punishment sent by God in response to people's initial refusal to heed the Word and to accept their opportunity for salvation.[3] Once spoken in the New World, the Word of God erased the legitimacy of previous religious practices and, significantly, exposed Aboriginal people to their ignorance as well as to the full force of the consequences of their sin. The words spoken by the Jesuits left a permanent mark, inhabiting the spaces where they had been spoken with a kind of ominous finality. To ignore them and the truths they announced was to make the fatal choice between salvation and condemnation to greater punishment in this life and the next. In a letter to Mutio Vitelleschi, general of the Society of Jesus at Rome, Lalemant explained: "While they were sound in body, they did not hear; it therefore pleased God to pull their ears through a certain kind of pestilence, which spread over the whole country, and adjudged many to the grave" (17:227).

At the beginning of the epidemics, Le Jeune compared the situation in which the priests found themselves with the persecution suffered by the first Christians and, reversing the accusations made against the Jesuits, attributed the diseases to God's justice: "All the misfortunes, all the pests, wars, and famines which in the early ages of the infant Church afflicted the world, were formerly attributed to the faith of Jesus Christ, and to those who embraced or preached it. What occurred in this regard in the primitive Church can be seen every day in new France, especially in the Huron country. There is no black malice of which we are not accused. Here are the causes of it. As the contagion caused a great many Hurons to die, these people, not recognizing therein the justice of God, who takes vengeance for their crimes, imagined that the French were the cause of their death" (12:85).

While the Jesuits attributed all power over the diseases to God and continually urged the Huron to have recourse to the faith, most Huron abandoned Christianity completely in an attempt to dissociate themselves from the priests' teachings and, by association, from the diseases. The few who had converted and who remained Christian during the epidemics were warned by their relatives of the injustice of the Jesuits' God and his powerlessness to assist them or to preserve their lives (19:211, 235). But while resistance to the Jesuits became more imperative for the majority of Huron men and women, it situated them in a more perilous position according to the Jesuits' understanding of the epidemic and its causes. The Huron's rejection of Christianity as the only possible cure and their continual search for cures among those offered by the shamans and curing societies confirmed the Jesuits' in their belief that the devil influenced these people's behaviour (15:71). According to this view, such behaviour made them more deserving of retribution for denying the opportunity for their salvation. In the same way, the threats and accusations that the Huron made against the priests – who believed themselves to be there as the instruments of the Huron's salvation – compounded the "measure of their sins" (13:161) and, consequently, the measure of their punishment. The Jesuits met the active resistance of the Huron with an intensification of their threats of punishment, rhetorically moving the Huron's refusal to comply into the realm of the worst blasphemy. While the Jesuits and many Huron apportioned blame for the disease to each other, they did so according to divergent cultural and ideological premises that enabled them to find significant, incontrovertible meaning in their respective actions. The result was a duel over signification, in which each became grist for the other's worst accusations as they struggled – if not for life and death itself – at least for the meaning of life and the cause of death.

The first serious outbreak of disease occurred during the autumn of 1636 and lasted through the winter. After this, the Jesuits moved their principal residence from the village of Ihonatiria, where many people had lost their lives to the disease, to the more southern and less afflicted village of Ossossané. The Jesuits had been publicly accused of practising witchcraft in Ihonatiria that winter and were aware that their lives were at risk. Le Mercier, the author of the Huron *Relation* for that year, identified one family as having been most active in these accusations. According to Le Mercier, it was when the priests' lives were most threatened that "the scourge fell upon that wretched family that had said the most against us. This chastisement had been for a long time due them on account of the contempt they had always shown for our holy mysteries" (13:217). Lalemant later explained that the move from Ihonatiria was necessary because its population was "nearly all ... scattered or dead from the malady, which seems to be, not without reason, a punishment from Heaven for the contempt that they showed for the favour of the visit that the divine goodness had procured for them" (17:11). The following autumn, when it appeared that a council of confederacy headmen in Ossossané would sanction the Jesuits' death, Brébeuf reiterated the priests' assumption that their lives would be preserved or disposed of solely as God willed. Their deaths would prevent the salvation of those they were trying to save, and Brébeuf believed that if God allowed the Jesuits to be killed, this in itself would be a form of punishment: "And yet I fear that divine Justice, seeing the obstinacy of the majority of these Barbarians in their follies, may very justly permit them to come and take away the life of the body from those who with all their hearts desire and procure the life of their souls" (15:63).

Crop failures, the escalation of the war with the Iroquois, and famines were also represented as the punishments of God. When Jérôme Lalemant described the destruction of one of the outlying Huron villages by an Iroquois war party, he associated this disaster with the village's previous rebelliousness: "It was the most impious of the villages, and that which had been most rebellious against the truths of the faith in all these countries; and its inhabitants had more than once told the Fathers who had gone to teach them that, if there were a God who avenged crimes, they defied him to make them feel his anger, and that, for anything less than that, they refused to acknowledge his power" (26:175). Similarly, Father Dequen explained to the Montagnais residing at Sillery that the capture of a group of Huron traders and the Jesuit father accompanying them, as well as "so many other misfortunes," were "the effects of God's anger, who was justly irritated by the wickedness of bad Christians and of the infidels who would not obey his word" (25:149).

Of course, the few who remained or became Christian during the epidemics were equally likely to suffer from the diseases. Similarly, as more people converted to Christianity after the diseases had run their course, they – like the non-Christians – were caught up in the punitive effects of escalating warfare and famine (25:105; 26:217). Inequities in the distribution of suffering are not unaccounted for in the Judeo-Christian tradition, and the Jesuits drew on well-established precedents when they represented these afflictions as having been sent by God for the improvement and redemption of those he had elected to save (26:217). Such was the argument offered to a group of Huron who complained that the Iroquois, who did not pray, were prospering and that since prayer had been introduced among the Huron, they themselves were perishing from warfare and disease. These Huron were told that God was behaving toward them "like a Father toward his child; if his child will not have sense, he punishes it, in order to give it some; having corrected it, he throws the rods into the fire. A Father does not put himself to so much trouble about his servants as about his

children. God regards you as his children: he wishes to give you
sense; he uses the Iroquois as a whip, in order to correct you, to
give you faith, to make you have recourse to him. When you shall
be wise, he will throw the rods into the fire; he will chastise the
Iroquois, unless they reform" (25:37).

The Jesuits had precedents for this language and did not have to
invent it for use in North America. However, such language
assumes particular potency when used in a situation of evolving
political and economic inequality, and in conjunction with what
was frequently an aggressive rhetoric of political imperialism,
which compared the spread of Christianity in the New World to a
territorial conquest. These Huron replied that they had enough
sense and suggested it might have been better if God had begun
with the Iroquois. The Jesuits advised them that their greater
misfortunes were due to the greater love God bore them and that,
however much the Iroquois appeared to be prospering, it was
certain that, as unbelievers, they would not enjoy the rewards of
the next life. The Jesuits' representation of suffering reflects an
assumption that the appropriate response to it could only be submission and endurance, undertaken with an understanding of the
presence of a superior will to which one must be subordinate, and
with the hope of rewards to come (Bowker 1970, 54). This complete abnegation of the self, along with submission before a greater
will, was a feature of the Jesuits' training. While the Jesuits' interlocutors frequently appeared unmoved by a God who apparently
benefited people through their affliction, for the Jesuits suffering
reduced neither the possibility of God nor the justice of God. Those
who endured with strength and patience would be recognized and
potentially rewarded – "for one is approved if, mindful of God, he
endures pain while suffering unjustly" (1 Peter 2:19).

When sent as trials, misfortunes were a tool for separating those
who were firm in the faith and willing to submit from those who
were not (32:189). It is significant that in the *Relations* these trials
were frequently represented as a necessary and important step in
the establishment of Christianity in North America, just as they
had been in Europe and Asia, where the faith of Christians had
been tested through political persecution. While describing the
hardships suffered by the Montagnais in the vicinity of Quebec, Le
Jeune asserted: "The Faith must propagate itself as it has been
planted, – namely, in calamities. And because there are here no

Tyrants who massacre our Neophytes, God provides for them otherwise, deriving proof of their constancy from their afflictions, sore indeed" (16:219). The repeated use of this historical reference situates the experiences of Native peoples in the St Lawrence region – for whom the signature events of Christianity were the remote occurrences in the life of an unknown prophet referring to the deity of an unknown people in a remote and alien land – within the frame of a universal, exclusively Christian and ultimately hegemonic vision of global history. In 1643 Barthélemy Vimont described the general condition of the Christians of New France:

The condition to which this nascent Church is now reduced is such as to bring to the eyes of all who love it tears both of sorrow and of joy. For, on the one hand, it is pitiful to see these poor peoples perish before our eyes as soon as they embrace the Faith; and, on the other, we have reason to console ourselves when we see that the misfortunes which assail them on all sides serve but to arouse a desire for the faith in those who had hitherto despised it, and to strengthen it and make it shine with still greater glory in the hearts of those who had already received it. We see very well that God is the Founder of this Church, as well as of the primitive one; for he has caused the former to be born, like the latter, in travails, and to grow in sufferings, in order to be crowned with her in glory. (25:105)

By the summer of 1649 most Huron villages had been destroyed or significantly depopulated by warfare and the accompanying famine and disease. The priests and surviving Huron took refuge on an island in Georgian Bay, where they were temporarily safe from Iroquois raiding parties but lacked provisions for the coming winter. "Then it was," according to Paul Ragueneau, that the missionaries "were compelled to behold dying skeletons eking out a miserable life, feeding even on the excrements and refuse of nature" (35:89). Conditions reached such an extreme that people were reduced to exhuming bodies for food. Ragueneau nevertheless wrote: "It was in the midst of these desolations that God was pleased to bring forth, from their deepest misfortunes, the well-being of this people. Their hearts had become so tractable to the faith that we effected in them, by a single word, more than we had ever been able to accomplish in entire years" (35:91).

The upheavals in Huron society in the final years of the Jesuits' mission among them made them more dependent on the Jesuits and enabled the priests to exact at least an outward compliance with Christianity. Lalemant had foreshadowed this role of affliction in creating subject relations of dependency, when he wrote of the general condition of Christianity in New France in the *Relation* for the years 1643–44: "We have, however, great reason to praise God because he reaps his glory from the affliction of these poor peoples and makes it serve still more for their conversion. Although there is not in the world a nation poorer than this one, nevertheless there is none prouder than they. When they were prosperous, we could hardly approach them; the French were dogs, and all that we preached them were fables. But since affliction has humiliated them, and necessity has made them more dependent upon the French, and has made them experience the effects of Christian charity, their eyes are opened; and they see more clearly than ever that there is no other Divinity than he whom we preach to them" (25:111). Lalemant's comment also reveals the strong sense of cultural superiority that characterized Aboriginal people's initial response to Europeans.

The Jesuits also represented affliction as the enactment of a more final and inevitable justice. In the Huron report of 1640 Lalemant explained that many "villages and cabins were much more populous formerly, but the extraordinary diseases and the wars within some years past, seem to have carried off the best portion; there remaining only very few old men, very few persons of skill and management" (19:127). To this he added, "It is to be feared that the climax of their sins is approaching, which moves divine justice to exterminate them as well as several other nations" (19:127). People who resisted conversion or actively argued against the Jesuits and who then suffered misfortune or death frequently figured in the *Relations* as examples of God's justice, however far removed this would have been from these people's own interpretation of their death or misfortune. The punishments featured in these incidents are in sharp contrast to the joy and gratitude which the Jesuits generally associated with conversion. In 1634 Paul Le Jeune attributed the miserable death of a "blasphemer" to the "just and terrible vengeance of the great God" (7:283). Ten years later Lalemant described the punishment of three Algonkin men who had come down to Trois-Rivières and were "placing some obstacles against the expansion of the Faith" by openly retaining more than one wife (31:257). Lalemant asserted that these three "refractory ones"

(31:257) were the victims of "a thunderbolt hurled from Heaven" (31:257), all dying ignoble or miserable deaths.

One of these men, on becoming ill, blamed Christianity and in so doing was said to have revolted "more than ever against the arm which struck him only to cure him" (31:263). The Jesuits warned him of the punishment that would come in the next life if he did not open his eyes and accept baptism, but he replied unrepentantly "that a Law which made men die was abominable" (31:261). He died in this refutation of the faith, a resistance that became, under Lalemant's pen, the "rage" that was "the Catastrophe of his life" (31:263). Another of these men especially annoyed the Jesuits by his persistence in attributing a recent outbreak of disease to the effects of Christianity, and when he too fell sick Lalemant described this as an attack by God (31:263). Lalemant referred to this man, who bore the name Joseph Oumosotiscouchie, as an apostate who was unusually "proud and insolent" because he had been given the name used by several former leaders in his country (31:261).

Oumosotiscouchie publicly denied the utility of prayer to heal, blaming his sickness on the faith, and he undertook to cure himself in a healing ceremony that involved the fulfilment of three dream wishes. On completion of the ceremony, he publicly claimed to be cured, at which point, according to Lalemant, "a violent fever seizes him in the midst of his triumph, prostrates him to the earth, throws him into a wreck and into torments so unusual that he foamed like one possessed. Those of his cabin – frightened, and fearing lest he might beat some one to death – having tied him, threw over him a blanket, so as to conceal his fury and his rage; behold my blusterer much humbled" (31:265). When the Jesuits and the surgeon arrived, they found the man "stone-dead" and all who had witnessed the event astonished at "so awful a spectacle" (31:265). This man was later "flung into a hole like a common sewer, for fear that he might infect the air with his body, as he had polluted it with his vices and his apostasy" (31:275). After this punishment, Lalemant stated with some satisfaction that no one "dared longer open his lips against the Faith; it was now spoken of only with a dread and respect that altogether pleased us" (31:267).[4]

Those who physically harmed Jesuits could also be situated in the *Relations* as victims of divine punishment. One man, for example, kicked a priest while the latter was baptizing a child, and "some time after that, he was carried off by a disease as grievous

as it was strange" (14:227). The woman who cut off the thumb of
Father Jogues while Jogues was a captive in an Iroquois village
apparently "had no long career after that rage" (29:229). Likewise,
wrote Lalemant: "They who gnawed his fingers and those of his
companions, and who treated them with most fury, have been killed
by the Algonquin in their latest combats" (29:229). The "same
justice" was applied to the Iroquois who tortured Father Bressani
when he was held captive among them, although this punishment
was in the form of diseases that would "perhaps ... give true health
to that poor people" (29:229).

THAT SHARP SWORD

The Jesuits in New France approved of the use of political authority
to support the missionary endeavour, and in this they were faithful
to the assumptions of the founder of their order. Ignatius Loyola
had taken for granted the state's ability and willingness to employ
military strength in support of missionaries (Aveling 1981, 153). In
Brazil, for example, Portuguese troops and Jesuit chaplains had
combined forces to undertake punitive expeditions to force indigenous people in the interior onto the Jesuit reductions (ibid., 154).
Half a century later in North America, Jérôme Lalemant expressed
regret that force could not be employed as effectively as it had been
in other missions: "We cannot here have force at hand, and the
support of that sharp sword which serves the Church in so holy a
manner to give authority to her Decrees, to maintain Justice, and
curb the insolence of those who trample under foot the holiness of
her Mysteries" (28:55). Many years later, in 1672, the Jesuit Jean
de Lamberville complained of the independence of the Iroquois,
among whom the Jesuits had begun missions, and suggested that
the only way they could be converted would be "to subdue them
to the faith by two arms, as it were – one of gold, and the other
of iron"; in other words, "to win them by presents, and to keep
them in subjection by the fear of arms" (57:127). But as he pointed
out, "Missionaries here have neither the attraction of the one nor
the strength of the other" (ibid.).[5]

Le Jeune was well aware that the authority of the faith was
connected to the strength of the French when he argued that the
"more imposing the power of our French people is made in these
Countries, the more easily they can make their belief received by

these Barbarians" (8:15). However, in the years prior to the destruction of the Huron mission, the power of the French was not as imposing as Le Jeune and the other Jesuits would have wished, even though Governor Montmagny supported the authority of the church and the priests with his political authority whenever possible (22:209). In the *Relation* of 1642, Vimont recorded the personal reprimand given by the governor to a non-Christian who had threatened the Christians at Sillery after the latter had prevented the man's son from courting one of their daughters. According to Vimont, Montmagny "bade his Interpreter tell" this man "that he must be very careful not to make any attempt against the Christians; that he could not attack them without attacking him personally; that he himself was but one with those who believe in JESUS CHRIST, and that he loved prayer" (22:125–7). Vimont confidently concluded that "such a sermon, preached in a Fort armed with a cannon, had its effect" (22:127).

A more politically significant incident occurred in 1640, when Montmagny punished, by unidentified means, some of the Huron traders who had arrived at Trois-Rivières that spring. The punishment was for threats and assaults that had been made against the Jesuits the previous winter (21:143). The winter of 1639–40 had been one in which the priests were accused of witchcraft, and the hostilities directed at them by many Huron men and women had been significant. Montmagny warned the traders that he would exact further penalties if any harm came to the Jesuits in the future. The traders took the governor's actions seriously, and many of them later offered the Jesuits reparation for the offences the priests had suffered throughout the winter (21:143). Lalemant approvingly reported on the "good effect" of what Montmagny had done, stating that the returned traders "did not less admire the wisdom of his conduct and of his justice in the past than they feared his menaces for the future" (21:143). In his view, this use of the governor's authority was "a pious employment of power to render it efficacious in maintaining in peace the Preachers of the Faith, in a country where impiety and insolence have reigned from the beginning of the world" (21:143).

Montmagny's treatment of the Huron traders in 1640 reveals the beginning of the kind of political and economic advantage which the French would increasingly enjoy in their relationship with the Huron. His actions would not have been possible even a few years earlier, when the French were as concerned as the Huron over the potential loss or interruption of their trading alliance (Trigger 1987, 597–8). Still, the French did not at that time have the power to rule by force in New France, and it is this kind of power that is generally understood to define colonialism (e.g., Young 1995, 165). The Jesuits were not unaware of the *realpolitik* of French economic and political efforts in North America, but the *Relations* continually gave voice to a vision of the inevitable sovereignty of church and crown in the New World. The language of the Christian mission was as frequently couched in a language of political imperialism as it was in the more benign idiom of agricultural processes. This language also legitimized both the colonizing and the Christianizing processes by referring to the unquestionable legitimacy of a Christian monarchy. In 1635 Le Jeune confidently declared: "The faith will banish infidelity from its Empire. It is, indeed, proper that in the Reign of so saintly a King, virtue should enter one of the great Seigniories of his Crown; that, under the favour and leadership of a Prince of the Church, we should see a new Church arise ... which shall extend its branches even to the sea, and shall propagate itself along the shores of the chief of rivers" (7:255).

In these early years, the French did not engage in wars of conquest on the St Lawrence, yet the *Relations* are replete with a rhetoric of conquest and possession in the name of a universal Christendom. A key feature of this rhetoric was the Jesuits' representation of themselves as soldiers of Christ, engaged in the liberation of a country ruled and oppressed by Satan – "the strong man armed who has commanded absolutely in this country during so many centuries" (17:19). Their portrayal of their missionary work in New France as a military endeavour was consistent with aspects of their training; the same approach had been used to characterize their work in Europe, Asia, and South America (Aveling 1981, 153). Ignatius Loyola had used military imagery to describe the organization and objectives of the Jesuit order. The Institutions he drafted for the regulation of the society and the Spiritual Exercises both reflected a view of future Jesuits as soldiers in the army of God, actively combatting the forces of evil. Loyola's emphasis was seconded by Pope Julius III in the papal bull authorizing the establishment of the Jesuits as a new order, in which the Jesuits were referred to as soldiers of God, or *militare deo* (Axtell 1985, 91). The Spiritual Exercises involved intensive meditations that were usually performed during a month-long period of retreat. All Jesuits were expected to take the exercises, first as initiates and then once a year for the rest of their careers. Notable among these meditations were the Two Standards, in which the initiate imagined Christ as "Commander-in chief" and Satan as "the mortal enemy," at the head of opposing armies, preparing to send their followers into the world (Fleming 1978, 84–90). The initiate then contemplated and prayed to be worthy to join those whom Christ had called to his standard (ibid., 88). Jesuits working in France used this imagery to support themselves in their missions to areas of Protestant influence (Grant 1984, 32).

"Soldier of God" had been a synonym for a member of a religious order since Medieval times, and it is possible to overstate the military emphasis of the Jesuits on the basis of the prominence of military imagery in Jesuit documents (O'Malley 1993, 45). Nevertheless, military metaphors did proliferate in the *Relations* from New France, where the "country of the Hurons, and other neighboring peoples" was itself "one of the principal fortresses and, as it were, a donjon of the Demons" (17:113). While the Jesuits' day-to-day lives may have been more mundane, in the *Relations* they represented their work in the dramatic terms of battle and conquest. In his first *Relation*, Le Jeune wrote that he came like one who went "ahead to dig the trenches," and he referred to the missionaries who would come after him as "brave soldiers" who would "besiege and take the place" (5:21). The priests engaged the support and prayers of their readers, telling them of "the combats and battles [they had] to give and sustain every day, in order to establish in this country a Sovereign other than he who, since all ages, had tyrannically usurped the empire of God and of Jesus Christ" (17:215). Their sermons and instruction, their plans to learn the languages, build hospitals, and settle hunting peoples such as the Montagnais were "the arms necessary for war" (17:9) and the "batteries" that would "destroy the empire of Satan, and ... unfurl the banner of Jesus Christ" (17:115; 14:127).[6]

As inhabitants of a usurped empire, the Huron, Montagnais, and other Native peoples who appeared in the *Relations* were described as living lives of miserable bondage. Their enslavement was to Satan, and the priests characterized it as "the strangest servitude and slavery that can be imagined ... Never did galley slave so fear to fail in his duty as these peoples dread to fall short in the least detail of all their wretched ceremonies" (17:161). The Jesuits described themselves as "wresting from [the Devil's] hands so many souls that he held captive" (14:51–3), a task made more difficult because the people were not aware of their captivity until they had been rescued. Jérôme Lalemant described one recently converted and baptized Huron, who was given the name Joseph, as "often imagining that he is like a prisoner of war in these quarters, escaped from the hands of his enemies, while his companions, bound with chains, are on the eve of suffering horrible torments; these are his own thoughts" (21:155). Another man was reported to have said, upon his decision to convert to Christianity, that it was "'time to submit." He added: "I have been fighting for two years; I must let myself be vanquished by God'" (22:109). The priests gave this man the name Victor and wrote that to "be vanquished in such a fight is to be victorious" (22:109). In this and other instances the Jesuits relied on the paradox, familiar in Christian tradition, whereby to lose all was to gain all. Liberation and true freedom came from submission to God and the Jesuits (22:105), while continuation in the "spirit of liberty" – decried by the Jesuits in so many contexts – only contributed to the bondage of sin.

The Jesuits' descriptions transformed the subjects of their mission into scenes of battle, conquest, and possession. This is the imagery employed by Father Lalemant when he wrote: "You see therein clearly, it would seem, the spirit of God and of the devil struggling in their minds and hearts. One day you see them all killing themselves to say that they believe, and that they wish to be baptized; another day, everything is overthrown and hopeless. This contrast is a manifest sign of combat and battle; but it must be confessed that we do not yet see to which side the complete victory leans" (17:125). Their language foreshadowed the spatial and ideological penetration of colonialism and mapped the mission on the territory of individual consciousnesses. Converts frequently experienced a significant transformation in personality and disposition after baptism; one man, for example, was changed "in such a way that one no longer knew him. A more disinterested Savage was never seen; he became pliable and humble, and tractable as a child" (31:283). The *Relations* suggest that these transformations were possible because of the potency of the Word and the power of God's grace to enter into and completely possess people's hearts and minds; ultimately, it was these that tamed and transformed savagery. In

1644 Lalemant recorded that "grace took possession" of one
woman's heart "and soon changed her nature," transforming her
"proud and mocking spirit" into one that was "all gentleness"
(27:49). True to the requirement that savagery was a recuperable
condition, the priests encouraged their readers not to be surprised
by "what the power of faith and of the divine grace can do when
it has gained possession of even Savage hearts" (24:107). Resistance
by the individual was futile, for there "are no hearts proof against
grace, when God wills to possess them" (31:181).

These themes of conquest and possession had legitimate precedents in Christian imagery and theology, and the Jesuits emphasized
this kind of total transformation of the individual in their approach
to conversion amongst themselves as well as in their missions
(O'Malley 1993, 70–1). However, the Jesuits' language is not innoc-
uous in the context of the early colonial endeavours of the French
state in North America, especially when they themselves linked the
mission with the sovereignty of the crown (7:225). While the Jesuits
who wrote between 1632 and 1650 did not live in a secure colony,
their language was the language of territorial expansion, and they
referred to both church and crown in amplifying this theme. The
Jesuits' emphasis on submission and obedience also derives from an
important aspect of Christian teaching, one with which they themselves were familiar. However, the language of obedience and submission in the *Relations* describes the desired relationship between
the Jesuits and people who are construed, through the Jesuits' discourse, as their inferiors; in so doing it expresses relations of domination and naturalizes them in relation to the tutelage that is the
obvious and necessary antidote to savagery and paganism.

The force of the inequality that this language speaks to is also
evident in the fact that submission could only be obtained by chas-
tisements that removed many people's political and economic
autonomy, forcing them onto the charity of the Jesuits and other
French. I do not suggest that political imperialism is an inevitable
consequence of Christianity or that Christian belief and Christian
themes are always used to naturalize relationships of power and
domination; although Christianity has been used in arguments supporting the conquest and domination of indigenous peoples by
force, it has also been used in some of the most trenchant critiques
of the abuses of power by Europeans in the New World (Greenblatt
1991, 70). The Jesuits' language, however, spoke to and justified

domination, and in so doing it both expressed and served an imperial theme. At the same time, part of its effect lay in its ability to familiarize and legitimize the events the Jesuits described. By using familiar themes and imagery, the Jesuits de-emphasized the political while transforming the suffering and disease experienced by Native people into manifestations of God's love, and transforming their freedom and independence into sinful pride and slavish servitude.

I have already suggested that there was little likelihood that those who converted to Christianity actually understood themselves to be so completely possessed or vanquished (cf. Grant 1984, 246). This is because the Huron, Montagnais, and other Native people among whom the Jesuits worked did not share the priests' assumption that religious truth was universal and consequently exclusive; thus they tended to incorporate the Jesuits' message into an existing spiritual repertoire. In this sense, Aboriginal people responded dialogically to the Jesuits' proclamations although, as we have seen, the *Relations* provided the Jesuits with a site where they could assert the truth in a more uncontested fashion. In addition, neither religious beliefs nor cultures – which cannot be separated from each other – are sets of ideas that are easily replaced, even in circumstances of upheaval. This degree of spiritual relativism, and its implications for the ability of beliefs to coexist, to inform each other, and to undergo resignification over time, was unacceptable to the Jesuits, who not only held to the assumption of Christian universalism but had made it their mission to accomplish this, whether in the European countryside or among the non-Christians of the Americas, Asia, and Africa. The invasive and domineering nature of their representations of conversion are based on the orthodox belief that Christian truth, as embodied by the Roman Catholic Church, could not share space with other beliefs – not within a state and certainly not within an individual.

There is some irony in the extent to which the idea of universalism is itself parochial (Comaroff and Comaroff 1992, 20). A considerable body of literature on colonialism demonstrates that there is less irony in the political consequences of the idea for colonized peoples; this literature also emphasizes the importance of a continuing critique of universalist logic and assumptions – both as it has been used in the past and as it continues to be used in the present. While the Jesuits made some concessions to cultural specificities and were undoubtedly more relativist than many other missionaries, they deployed an unremittingly universalist vision in New France. Their labour was, first and foremost, in the name of "Jesus Christ, who must finally subjugate all the world" (20:77). Le Jeune explained that the Montagnais, Huron, and all other Aboriginal inhabitants of New France were obligated, "together with all the Nations of the earth" (8:167), to the sacrifice Christ had made for them.[7] The Jesuits' understanding of the country and people of North America as the rightful heritage of Christ contributed to the rhetoric of conquest and possession that characterized the *Relations*. In 1640 Le Jeune confidently affirmed the righteousness of the Christianizing mission: "We cannot call in question the truth that the Eternal Father wishes to put his Son into possession of the heritage that he has provided him ... He shall rule from the North sea to the South sea ... and from the great river St. Lawrence, which is the chief of all rivers, to the remotest confines of the earth, even to the farthest boundaries of America and to the Islands of Japan ... and beyond ... All the nations shall render him homage ... He shall save the souls of the poor Savages ... All peoples shall magnify him ... His Majesty shall fill all the earth; *fiat, fiat*" (18:239).

Conclusion

In 1644 Jérôme Lalemant defended the Jesuits' slow progress in their missions in New France by writing: "As faith is not natural to these peoples, – as it seems to be in France, where it is imbibed with one's mothers' milk, – it is not a mere trifle to have made a man a Christian. More contests, more pains, and more labors are needed to retain and keep him in the Church than were required to win him to God" (28:55). This comment reveals the considerable difficulties the Jesuits encountered as they tried to convert Aboriginal people to Christianity, and as they tried to keep these converts. Lalemant wrote the comment in the letter to his superior in Paris which I have cited in previous chapters. The Jesuits did not always reveal such difficulties; indeed, the language they used in the *Relations* was generally more confident. Throughout this book I have argued that this language did not represent the impact which the Jesuits' teaching actually had on Native people in the Northeast during the first half of the seventeenth century. I have argued that the invasive metaphors of conversion, and the Jesuits' association of conversion with conquest and submission, were powerful rhetorical forms, implicated in a vision of asymmetrical social and political relationships in which Aboriginal people were to be subordinated to the Jesuits. While descriptions of conversion involved some of the most imperialist and oppressive language in the *Relations*, I have argued that the conquest and incorporation of the converted Christian subject represented by such passages was more literary than literal – occurring primarily in the rhetorical universe of the *Relations*, and effective in this way in situating Aboriginal people as vanquished and obedient subjects.

The Jesuits' metaphors also took their meaning from a culturally situated understanding of conversion; because of this, too, they cannot be seen as direct reflections of individual Aboriginal people's understanding of that same process and its effects. While much of the language in the *Relations* rhetorically situates Native people as passive objects, to be acted on with the power of the Word and brought into history by an agency external to themselves, I have argued that this positioning belies the presence of Native peoples as historical actors whose cultural logics were capable of decentring the Jesuits' message and challenging and subverting the Jesuits' authority. In doing so, I have tried to show that the encounter between Jesuits and Aboriginal peoples was a process of engagement and struggle, resulting in intersecting meanings, altered significances, and the emergence of a complex web of relationships between the actors involved. I have also suggested that the struggle over signification that characterized the Jesuits' attempts to convince people to convert to Christianity resulted in fissures and unexpected and uncontrollable conceptual slippage, and that this made the Jesuits' attempt to impose a new hegemony impossible.

Lalemant's comment also suggests that although Christianity – in this case, seventeenth-century reformed Catholicism – was institutionalized in forms of external, visible ritual that appeared separable from everyday life, it was in fact as socially and culturally embedded as the religious beliefs of Aboriginal peoples. The Jesuits were generally tolerant of local customs in their mission work around the globe, and I have pointed out that this was the approach they initially brought to their mission in New France. The difficulties they met in the absence of concurring or compatible interpretations of authority and punishment, however, eventually prompted them to make more concerted attempts to impose elements of a cultural context, which they, for all their occasional relativism, could not identify as human invention. This was reflected in their emphasis on the efficacy of punishment and the necessity of hierarchy and obedience in social and political orders that set the terms of an individual's relationship with God. It was also reflected in their desire to encourage hierarchical social relations and punitive practices in Aboriginal communities.

At the same time, the Jesuits never completely agreed with or adopted the policy advocated by the Recollets who had preceded them as missionaries on the St Lawrence. The Recollets had based their approach to conversion on the assumption that Native people could only be made Christian after they had settled among French people and been taught their language, manners, and customs (Trigger 1987, 468). The Jesuits did not foresee a similar need for such wholesale assimilation and did not attempt it, even after realizing the extent to which Aboriginal religious beliefs were intertwined with Aboriginal cultures. They continued to adapt Native customs to Christian ritual and to learn and use Native languages in their missions throughout the seventeenth century. Even after 1667, when the French government tried to promote new attempts to encourage Aboriginal people to live among French settlers and adopt the French language and habits, in the hope that this would encourage more settlement in the colony, the Jesuits put little faith in the success of such attempts (Trigger 1985, 294).

During the time dealt with in this study, the Jesuits combined a policy of coercion with one of relative accommodation. This combination reveals the tension between relativism and universalism which, I suggest, was characteristic of their mission in New France. I draw attention to this here because this combination, no less than their accounts of their work and their views of Native people as recorded in the *Relations*, reveals the complexity involved in the creation and perception of difference in this as in other colonial encounters. This complexity in turn speaks to the absence of rigid dichotomies between colonizers and the colonized (or the soon-to-be colonized) that I emphasized at the beginning of this book. The idea of such a dichotomy pervades colonial discourses themselves, where the differences between Aboriginal populations and the colonial newcomers are emphasized and are in part maintained and reinforced through their repeated articulation. This othering is an essential ideological manoeuvre in colonial discourses and an ideological support of colonialism itself, as Dirks explains: "Before places and peoples could be colonized, they had to be marked as foreign, as other, as colonizable" (1992a, 6).

These dichotomies have been taken up and echoed – in ways that both reproduced colonial categories and challenged the hierarchies that such categories supported – by many of the colonized, informing the nationalist independence movements that challenged colonial rule.[1] By emphasizing boundaries, colonial authors revealed an anxiety about them. If boundaries were permeable and could be blurred through intermingling and intermarriage, rulers would be left with no claims for either their superiority or the legitimacy of their rule (Cooper and Stoler 1997, 5). Their emphasis on the differences between themselves and the "natives" also suggests that the distinctions they wrote about were not always self-evident – however much the rhetoric suggested they should be – but, rather, had to be worked on in the course of everyday life in many colonies. These distinctions were thus not just a product of discourse but a matter of practice.

It is significant that when the first Jesuits arrived in the St Lawrence Valley in 1625, they came with the power to have the interpreters barred from living among the people they were trying to convert (Trigger 1987, 404–5). Etienne Brûlé was one such interpreter; he and others practised their Catholicism in a minimal fashion, if at all, and were generally happy to live among their Native hosts according to Native customs. When the Jesuits returned in 1632, they not only maintained this policy but were able to extend it to include independent traders, who similarly spent months at a time living with Aboriginal groups such as the Huron and the neighbouring Nipissing and Algonkin (ibid., 470–1). The Jesuits found the presence of such men problematic, as had the Recollets before them, because it exposed Aboriginal people to examples of what the priests could only consider to be lax morals. These examples contradicted the Jesuits' teaching and undermined their authority (6:83). Their need to ban these men from the proximity of their missions, allowing only those laypeople who were under their control and could be prevented from becoming "debauched among the Indians" (6:83), proves the point that the boundary between the French – who did not exist as a homogeneous category – and what the Jesuits identified as savagery and paganism was not necessarily a given but, for the Jesuits at least, was a distinction that had to be worked upon. It also suggests, of course, the extent to which the Jesuits' teaching referred to an ideal of Christian behaviour that was not shared by many of the French.

Cooper and Stoler (1997, 8) have recently written that "the Manichaean world of high colonialism that we have etched so deeply in our historiographies was … nothing of the sort." A much more nuanced appreciation of colonialism can emerge when we consider the range of distinctions that have been made in different colonies at different times, according to such things as class, nationality, gender, race, or degrees of blood. The task of identifying these

more complex social taxonomies, as well how they were produced
and how they changed over time, is difficult, however. The *Jesuit
Relations* were not the product of the high colonialism of the
nineteenth and twentieth centuries to which Cooper and Stoler
– and, indeed, many contemporary critics of colonialist discourse –
primarily refer. They nevertheless document a complex and contradictory process, in which the distinctions between Christian civilization and savagery were identified and defined in terms that were
often rigid – but were then blurred through the course of attempted
conversion and the accidents of translation. This is because the
Jesuits tried to engage Native people in a conversation leading to
conversion. In this way, the distinctions that were elaborated in
print were in some sense subverted through practice. The Jesuits
had to describe Aboriginal people in a way that demanded their
intervention as missionaries. The Native inhabitants of the
St Lawrence region thus emerged from the Jesuits' texts as *les
sauvages*, men and women who were lost to time as well as to the
temptations that their independent and unrestrained wills could not
refuse, living in forests in ways more appropriate to animals than
humans, being brutal in some of their habits, yet vulnerable and
at times even pitiable as they teetered on the abyss between salvation and damnation. The Jesuits created a category of difference
that could not be left as difference and was, on the whole, cast in
terms of inequalities that further legitimated the Jesuits' intervention and their assumption of authority over Native peoples.

They also, like so many who described the Others of Europe's
colonial encounters, created a category of difference that was
knowable. I have already noted that the Jesuits did not organize
difference according to the notion of culture, but that they did
search for and expect to find customs, traits, and manners that
were permanent and by which the people they wrote about could
be identified. In doing this, the Jesuits assumed that the assemblage
of characteristics they were trying to identify was ontologically
given – that it had a fixed and identifiable form that did not change
and needed only to be discovered to be known. The Jesuits'
accounts of these customs and manners were systematic and carefully supported with evidence of their physical, witnessing presence
– evidence that established their authorial credibility and lent
greater legitimacy to their descriptions. At the beginning of his
second *Relation*, Le Jeune expressed his concern for accuracy of

description, writing that although he had been "told many different things about the customs of these tribes," he would have "time enough to learn how true they [were]" (5:115). His point is that with time and experience in the country, he would be able to produce an informed and accurate account of indigenous ways of life and habits. The Jesuits' pursuit of knowledge about Aboriginal customs can be linked to their authoritative descriptions. This is because the Jesuits represented in their *Relations* the knowledge they sought in the hope of acquiring greater authority and influence over Aboriginal peoples, and by so doing they established their authority and credibility as authors to their European audience.[2]

As the Jesuits' emphasized the ahistoric state of the land and people of the Northeast, they also, as we have seen, described Native customs as static and unchanging over time, thereby lodging Native people in a category that was fixed and from which generalizations could be made. More specifically, although the Jesuits did distinguish between peoples such as the Huron and the Montagnais, as well as the Iroquois and others, one of the effects of their descriptions of Native ways was to establish the category of savagery as knowable and predictable. This category included what may currently be recognized as ethnographically correct descriptions of rituals, governance, and subsistence technologies, many of which could be identified with specific peoples. It also included the characteristics that were more definitive of savagery generally, such as liberty, the absence of effective or punitive governments, and the inability to overcome sensual appetites. In this – as in all reductive discourses – the particular disappeared in favour of a generalized representative subject. When Le Jeune used the behaviour of a few individuals as an example of what he considered to be the absence of charity among the Montagnais, he summed up by saying, "From this sample, judge of the whole piece" (6:259).[3]

This way of writing about and perceiving an other is based on reified notions of custom or culture, and is given to the essentialist logic of stereotypes. Once traits are determined as characteristic, they become self-fulfilling and self-perpetuating. Customs, manners, and morality become established as the truth, or as what may be expected, and are then represented without question. When the Jesuits attempted to establish a seminary for Huron boys, Le Jeune reported that their first pupils gave "themselves up, according to their custom, to thieving, gormandizing, gaming, idleness, lying, and similar irregularities" (14:233). In writing this, Le Jeune was relying on the already existing general depiction of unbridled liberty in the *Relations* as well as on the idea of custom, by which habits could be explained, predicted, or simply identified, to account for these boys' apparently unscholarly behaviour.

The Jesuits' writing of the category of savagery thus had the effect of fixing difference in a way that is comparable to the effects of other colonial discourses (Bhabha 1994, 66). There is a relationship between the process of rendering difference – according to notions of civilization and savagery such as those used in the *Relations*, or according to race, gender, culture, and nationality – and the ideologies that have supported various colonialisms. The elaboration of differences according to discrete categories has been combined with essentializing modes of representation that fix alterity in such a way that it can always be known, with the consequence that individuals may always be interpreted as representative of more general, predictable types. I have already pointed out that one of the objectives of colonial discourse studies is to identify these categories, to situate them in the multiple contexts and consequences of their production, and to show, through a critique of the content and forms of the language used, how they are naturalized. This task involves demonstrating how something such as "the primitive" or "the Oriental" can be rendered, through the terms and strategies of language, as something that exists naturally and to which descriptive language is merely applied, rather than as something that is constructed through language in specific social and political contexts. This endeavour is also based on the principle that while the social taxonomies informing colonial discourses may be invented, they are located in concrete social, political, and economic contexts. They thus have real consequences for people, determining who, for example, may be subject to slavery or other forms of violence, who may have their lands dispossessed or their children removed, or who indeed may inherit land and vote (Cooper and Stoler 1997, 6).

In my examination of the content of the category of savagery, I have shown that it is not a descriptive term used to label an existing empirical reality; it is a cultural artifact, embedded in a complex historical, cultural, and religious framework and is understandable only through historical and cultural analysis. Although the category was constructed, it is powerful both in its claim to describe reality and in its existence as a taken-for-granted category to which specific characteristics can be ascribed and from which relationships of inequality and tutelage can naturally follow. However, while the descriptions of savagery in the *Relations* rhetorically subordinated Native peoples to the Jesuits and emphasized boundaries and dichotomous oppositions, the nature of the Jesuits' purpose as missionaries and their own particular approach to that purpose involved them in always trying to bridge the opposition which they perceived and described. The Jesuits had to define a boundary in order to locate the savage and the pagan – the object and rationale of their mission. They then had to step out of and across this boundary in order to try to convert people to Christianity – without, however, simply attempting to create French men and women out of the Native converts. By casting their message according to their understanding of Aboriginal languages and customs – a process which, as I have argued, resulted in considerable conceptual slippage and intermingling of meaning – they perpetually interfered with this boundary. The Jesuits' claim to power and moral authority, and their sweeping assertions of the truth, were also challenged and were in many ways subverted as Aboriginal people struggled with the priests over the meaning of events, as well as the meaning of life and death.

Another objective of colonial discourse studies is to link to the present the categories and themes that served domination in the past, addressing how such categories continue to inform and are reshaped within present circumstances. In the case of the material I have analysed in this book, these linkages are not always immediately apparent, even though they may seem so. Unlike many of the colonial texts that have become the object of contemporary critical scrutiny, the *Relations* were written before the European Enlightenment – before the emphasis on science and reason, and the link between them and the notion of progress; before the secularization that displaced the sovereignty of the church and the dominant religious interpretations of humankind's place in the world; and before Darwin and the rise of evolutionary theories that encouraged interpretations of colonized peoples as close to animals in ways that were quite different from those advanced by the Jesuits. The Jesuits' principal categories were of savagery, which was pagan, and Christianity, which they linked to civilization. These were categories of the early modern age, but while they were no longer medieval, they were not those of the disenchanted, secularized Europe that was to come. The Jesuits' categories do not have as much salience today; indeed, they have been almost entirely displaced by the discourses of rights, self-determination, citizenship, and culture that currently frame public debates between indigenous peoples and the state in Canada and elsewhere. These debates are embedded in and informed by the ideological inheritance of the Enlightenment, and they would be alien in many of their concepts – although not in the fact that they are attempts to determine the nature and consequences of the difference between indigenous and non-indigenous peoples – to the Jesuits with whom I have dealt in this analysis.

The Jesuits' texts have, however, informed generations of historians of New France and Canada, and images of savages and martyred priests have been essential components of the historiography of this period and of the national consciousnesses in both English and French Canada (Trigger 1985, 6, 226). While these images may no longer be sanctioned in official public discourses, they have not vanished from the social imaginary or from the contemporary non-Native understanding of the historical relationships between Europeans and Native peoples on this continent (Sioui 1992, ix–xx). They have been, and remain, available for appropriation. However, what must be emphasized is that these appropriations always occur in terms that are specific to the present. The images and logic of the Jesuits are not so much repeated as they are layered over with the ideological accretions of a discontinuous history. Writing in the nineteenth century, the Protestant historian Francis Parkman deplored the Jesuits' religious beliefs, yet he depicted the Jesuits as heroic missionaries and represented indigenous people as rude savages. While in this respect Parkman reproduced certain themes of the Jesuits, he also described Aboriginal peoples, no less than the French and the English who came to North America, in terms of race and nationality. These ideas had a specific prominence in the nineteenth century and, with their strong biological undercurrents, would have been alien to the Jesuits.

Parkman's work is a now obvious example of the degree to which interpretations and representations of Aboriginal people in historiography have been problematic, yet Parkman advised his readers that "the closest examination" had assured him that the Jesuits "wrote in perfect good faith, and that the *Relations* hold a high place as authentic and trustworthy historical documents" ([1867] 1927, vi). The results of Parkman's descriptions were in some

ways more derogatory than the Jesuits' own understanding of
humanity and the place of Aboriginal peoples within it. While the
Jesuits evoked the absence of history, they did not write about the
absence of progress and did not link this absence to the biological
determinants of race and the place of different peoples on an
evolutionary scale.

In more contemporary times, remnants of the idea of the noble
savage are sometimes evident in popular images of indigenous
people. This idea can be traced in part through Enlightenment
thinkers of the eighteenth century to some of the Jesuits' descriptions of the absence of corruption and the potential for achieving
spiritual purity in the woods, far from the distractions of a mate-
rialist civilization (e.g., 32:283ff). Current appeals to this image are
also heavily influenced by nostalgia for a time before the environmental depredations of industrialization and the alienation of
industrial labour, as well as for a time of harmony between humans
and the natural world. This nostalgia and longing for a simpler
and more environmentally sound past were wholly uncharacteristic
of the Jesuits' pre-industrial, pre-romantic writings.

The legacy of the Jesuits' representations and of the age that
generated them seem both immediate and remote, present in the
images of the past and in some contemporary images of Aboriginal
peoples, but wholly absent in others. To the extent that they are
present, they are layered over with the ideas of other ages and other
purportedly fixed and certain knowledge, knowledge that is as
much a cultural artifact as that of the Jesuits. The Jesuits' certitude
of the universal validity of their beliefs permeates their texts and
supported them in their labours. When they were accused of witchcraft by the people they had thought to save from damnation, they
resorted to truths they believed to be fixed and immutable, and
stood firm in their knowledge of something that was universal and
unchanging. Part of my purpose has been to remove these closures
in the Jesuits' discourse, questioning both the truths to which the
Jesuits' adhered and those they created, as well as their depictions
of their own authority and power. I also intended to juxtapose the
specificity of their outlook with their universalist assumptions.

By emphasizing the specificity of the Jesuits' descriptions of
Aboriginal people – descriptions that were based on ideas of savagery and paganism rather than, for example, on race or underdevelopment – I aimed to highlight the complexity of colonialism and

the ideas that have informed it. I mention underdevelopment here because, since the Second World War, development has taken the place of civilization in many representations of the non-Western world. As I have tried to emphasize throughout this work, my analysis was based on the principle that colonialisms differ and cannot be reduced to any one essential logic. My goal has also been to draw attention to the constructedness of the categories through which the colonizers and the colonized have been represented – and to some extent continue to imagine each other – as well as the relationship of the knowledge that is produced about each to structures of domination. The certainties of any age and of any people can be the fictions and superstitious nonsense of another; the *Relations* make this clear both in the Jesuits' responses to Aboriginal people and in the Jesuits' own, historically locatable categories. The point is to encourage critical appraisal of such certainties and the balance of power that accompanies them. This seems especially important in our current globalized era, where an emphasis on diversity and multiculturalism in some Western nations exists alongside a more powerful narrative of modernization and progress. This narrative is part of the story we tell ourselves about ourselves, but it implies an opposite, which is about backwardness, underdevelopment, and the failure to throw off the yokes of tradition and superstition in order to move forward. In its totality, the narrative expresses a hierarchy similar to the hierarchy between savagery and civilization.

The Jesuits were able to combine a policy of cultural relativism with an overriding certainty of the legitimacy of certain truths and coercive intentions to change Aboriginal people's ways of life. It is perhaps fitting to conclude our reflections on the social situatedness of perception with a comment of Jérôme Lalemant's, who was possibly one of the most dogmatic of the Jesuits who wrote the early *Relations*. Lalemant stated, with no irony but apparently some pity: "These poor people – who have never seen anything but forests, rivers and mountains; who have conversed only with Caribous, Elks, and Beavers – conceive things only in their own manner" (31:247).

Notes

1 This practice of sending reports of varying degrees of formality home from the mission field was standard procedure among the Jesuits, who had been active in Europe, Asia, and South America prior to their arrival in North America (Correia-Afonso 1980, 11); not all of these reports and letters, however, were intended for publication in the way the *Relations* were.

2 Thwaites (1896–1901, 1:41) has attributed the cessation of the *Relations* publication in 1673 to the political influence of Frontenac, the governor of New France, with whom the Jesuits were in frequent conflict over policies relating to the mission and the use of alcohol in the fur trade. Lawrence Wroth (1936, 130), however, has suggested that this interpretation is incorrect. He attributes the sudden ending of the *Relations* publication to the Jesuits' response to a decree that was issued by the Congregatio de Propaganda Fide in Rome in 1672 and authorized by the pope in 1673. This decree prohibited the publication of all writings on missionary activities without the written authorization of the Propaganda itself (ibid., 132–3). According to Wroth, the difficulty for the Jesuits in France lay in the Parlement of Paris, which at that time did not recognize the authority of the Roman Congregation. The authorization required by Rome would not be permitted in a book published in France, yet to publish the books without the authorization would have meant excommunication from Rome as a penalty for the disobedience.

3 For example, Anderson 1991; Axtell 1985; Beaulieu 1990; Campeau 1987; Delâge 1993; Heidenreich 1971, 1978; Jaenen 1976;

Jetten 1994; Leacock 1980, 1981; Morrison 1985, 1986, 1990; Sioui 1994; Steckley 1992; Tooker [1964] 1991; Trigger 1987.

4 As a term describing a distinct and bounded set of traits and beliefs possessed by nations and crucial to their claims of historical and political legitimacy, culture was not a concept that was relevant either for Jesuits or for Aboriginal peoples in the early seventeenth century. In the seventeenth century, "culture" had not yet assumed usage as a noun referring to ways of life; instead, it denoted the tending of things, primarily crops or animals (Williams 1988, 87). This meaning of husbandry was gradually extended by metaphor to human development, and these were the two main senses of culture until the late eighteenth and early nineteenth centuries (ibid.; see also Wagner 1975, 21). In French, the occasional use of "culture" as an independent noun began later than in English, dating from the mid-eighteenth century (Williams 1988, 88–9). In the nineteenth century a humanist notion of culture prevailed, in which culture was both synonymous with civilization and referred to the best in social, creative, and intellectual achievement. According to this understanding, culture was still very much singular. It was the opposite of savagery as well as the common vulgarity of the masses; in this sense, it was possessed in greater or lesser degrees by different societies as well as by different classes within them. The more relativistic anthropological concept of culture, conceived in the plural and referring to whole ways of life, emerged only in the early twentieth century. While the earlier humanist views of culture continue to be apparent in the contemporary association between culture and the creative arts, the anthropological concept did enter more general usage as an alternative to the prevailing racial classifications of human difference (Clifford 1988, 234). Many discourses that employ culture while deploring race implicitly ascribe to cultural differences a similar kind of innateness, thereby approaching the biological determinist arguments that were and continue to be so offensive in racial typologies (Gilroy 1987).

5 The use of speeches attributed to indigenous people as a literary device – as a tool to achieve a particular effect – was also common. European authors frequently produced the negative reaction of New World peoples to European social mores and practices as a means of criticizing such practices (Jaenen 1974, 285). This was a useful method of indirect criticism when a more direct approach would have been socially and politically dangerous. However, such speeches

more frequently reflected the opinions of their European authors than of any indigenous interlocutor (ibid.).

6 This is Steckley's translation of the original Huron. The documents to which Steckley refers include a catechism, *De religione*, as well as *Instructions d'un infidel moribond*, which provided a guide for the instruction of a dying "pagan." They were copied by the Jesuit Father Pierre Potier during the mid-eighteenth century and first published in 1920, untranslated, under Potier's name, in *The Fifteenth Report of the Bureau of Archives for the Province of Ontario for the Years 1918–1919*.

7 Describing the Attikamegues, a people who lived in the northern Saguenay region and made periodic visits to Trois-Rivières, Father Lalemant wrote: "It seems as if innocence, banished from the majority of the Empires and Kingdoms of the World, had withdrawn into these great forests where these people dwell. Their nature has something, I know not what, of the goodness of the Terrestrial Paradise before sin had entered it. Their practices manifest none of the luxury, the ambition, the avarice, or the pleasures that corrupt our cities. Since Baptism has made them disciples of the Holy Ghost, that Doctor is pleased to be with them; he teaches them, far from the noise of tribunals and of Louvres; he has made them more learned, without books, than any Aristotle ever was with his ponderous volumes" (32:283). After giving some evidence of the goodness of these people, Lalemant went on to say, in keeping with the assumptions about women that permeated his era, that "what seems quite astonishing is, that the women are in no respect behind the men" in the performance of their Christian duties (32:289).

8 Indeed, it would be possible to use material taken from the *Relations* alone, or in conjunction with other colonial texts describing North and South America, to create a utopian picture of Aboriginal societies. To do so, however, would be to overlook the social, cultural, and political contexts of the texts in question. A number of European authors constructed utopian and idealistic images of life in the New World in order to comment on European society; they did this in reference to, and in the context of, the contemporary European debates over the nature of humankind, civilization, and morality (Jaenen 1974, 285; Tooker 1994, 310). Images of the people of North and South America as uncorrupted and morally superior (in opposition to images of the same peoples as depraved and not quite human) were entered into these debates as instruments in arguments

whose meaning originated in Europe, with little reference to the real complexities or nuances of life as it was variously lived by indigenous people in North and South America (Dickason 1984, 82).

9 Jean de Brébeuf accompanied his account of the Huron belief in the prophetic power of dreams with an assurance of first-hand knowledge: "Moreover, let no one think I make herein an amplification or exaggeration at pleasure; the experience of five years, during which I have been studying the manners and usages of our Savages, compels me to speak in this way" (10:71). In 1637 Father Pijart more directly drew on eyewitnessing to support his account of a Huron *Aoutaerohi*. This was a feast held by a curing society whose members were known for their ability to handle fire, including taking red-hot stones in their mouths without suffering injury (Trigger 1987, 80). Pijart reported that these "incredible" (14:59) features of the feast were true, writing, "You may believe me since I speak of a thing that I saw with my own eyes" (14:59). The testimony of "I have seen" had long been essential to European discourses of travel writing and owes its powers of persuasion to the early association between witnessing and knowledge in Indo-European languages (Hartog 1988, 261). Herodotus used personal experience and eyewitnessing to vouch for the credibility of his descriptions of the world beyond the cities of Greece. This was one of the first uses of the rhetoric of eyewitnessing as a key discursive strategy in descriptions of foreign lands and peoples (Greenblatt 1991, 122–3). The legitimating effect of eyewitnessing, as observation, became equally important in establishing ethnographic authority in the nineteenth and twentieth centuries (Crapanzano 1986, 57).

10 On imperialist nostalgia, see Rosaldo (1989, 68ff) and Rushdie (1991, 92).

11 E.g., Berthiaume 1988; Dickason 1984; Ferland 1992, 1993; Gagnon 1984; Laflèche 1988, 1989; Le Bras 1994; Ouellet 1987, 1993; Pioffet 1993.

12 Le Jeune wrote: "Their children will be as so many hostages to us for the safety of the French who are among them, and for the strengthening of our commercial relations" (9:283).

13 "The children of allies are no longer children but, whether they like it or not, are prisoners."

14 Champlain's diplomacy stands in considerable contrast to the precedent set by Jacques Cartier in the early sixteenth century. Unlike Champlain, who actually made exchanges, Cartier forcibly abducted

people, taking them back to France against their will (Trigger 1987, 199). He was unaware of the principles of such exchanges, and, given his actions, would have been uninterested in them even if they could have been made known to him. A number of the people he took never returned to North America. These and other high-handed actions on the part of Cartier led to bad faith and overt hostilities between himself, his men, and the Iroquoians who inhabited the St Lawrence Valley in the mid-sixteenth century.

CHAPTER TWO

1 The broad outline of historical events relating to the beginnings of New France contained in the first half of this chapter relies primarily on Trudel (1973) and Lanctot (1963).

2 Loyola's specific words in the Constitutions of the Society were: "The end of this Society is to devote itself with God's grace not only to the salvation and perfection of the members' own souls, but also with that same grace to labor strenuously in giving aid toward the salvation and perfection of the souls of their fellowmen" (Constitutions [3], translated by George E. Ganss, SJ).

3 The Formula of the Society of Jesus explains that the purpose of the society is "to strive especially for the defense and propagation of the faith and for the progress of souls in Christian life and doctrine, by means of public preaching, lectures, and any other ministration whatsoever of the word of God, and further by means of the Spiritual Exercises, the education of children and unlettered persons in Christianity, and the spiritual consolation of Christ's faithful through hearing confessions and administering the other sacraments." This formula appeared in the papal bull *Exposcit debitum* of 21 July 1550 (Ganss 1970, 63, 66–7).

4 One of the more enduring stereotypes associated with the Society of Jesus is that of the Jesuit as especially skilled at court intrigue and the manipulation of political influence. The practice of cultivating the interest of potentially powerful people had in fact been recommended by Loyola in the Constitutions of the Society (Martin 1973, 21). Many Jesuits did become closely associated with monarchs, often as their confessors, as well as with other influential people. That they did so and willingly used these connections to their advantage was not unusual behaviour, either generally or for members of a religious order in particular (Aveling 1981, 229–33). Nor was this

activity representative of the order as a whole, for most Jesuits worked in relative obscurity.

5 One of the most important rationales for a strong and powerful monarch in fact rested on the greater ability of a secure sovereign to fulfill his obligation to protect his subjects from the abusive powers of others, both from within the realm and without.

6 Throughout this book I use the names historically given to Aboriginal groups by Europeans, such as Montagnais and Huron. These two Aboriginal nations self-identify as Innu and Wendat, respectively. The conventional terms are, however, the terms used by the Jesuits, from whose texts I liberally quote, and I have chosen to retain them in order to avoid confusion.

7 In the seventeenth century, the members of this confederacy were the Mohawk, Oneida, Onandaga, Cayuga, and Seneca, all living in the area of what is now upper New York State. These five were joined in the eighteenth century by the Tuscarora.

8 The terms Algonkin and Algonkian, with the variant spellings Algonquin and Algonquian, require clarification. Algonkian has been used to denote a family of languages spoken over a broad region of northeastern and central North America (Day and Trigger 1978, 792). Algonkin comes from a Maliseet word meaning "they are our relatives (or allies)," and refers to the people inhabiting the area of the Ottawa Valley and regions to the east, all of whom were Algonkian speakers (ibid.). During the first half of the seventeenth century the Jesuits did not focus any concerted missionary activity on the Algonkin in the Ottawa Valley. Algonkin individuals and families did, however, travel to and live in or near various settlements along the St Lawrence, including Sillery, Tadoussac, and Trois-Rivières, where they encountered the Jesuits and were exposed to their teaching.

9 Le Jeune hoped that Pierre would assist him both to learn the language and to translate his Christian teachings to the group. However, Pierre not only refused to do so but further frustrated Le Jeune by denying and deriding Christianity. Pierre's position among the families appears to have been marginal, and his hostility toward the priest seems to have been attributable in some measure to the influence of Carigonan (Grassmann 1966, 533). Le Jeune described Pierre as an apostate and severely castigated him in print. Pierre died of starvation in the woods in 1636.

10 "Believe me, if I have brought back no other fruits from the Savages, I have at least learned many of the insulting words of their language.

They were saying to me at every turn ... 'Shut up, shut up, thou hast no sense' ... 'He is proud' ... 'He plays the parasite' ... 'He is haughty' ... 'He looks like a Dog' ... 'He looks like a Bear' ... 'He is bearded like a Hare' ... 'He is Captain of the Dogs' ... 'He has a head like a pumpkin' ... 'He is deformed, he is ugly' ... 'He is drunk'" (7:61–3).

CHAPTER THREE

1 Genesis 3:17–19, 23.

2 Several years earlier, Marc Lescarbot had similarly reflected on the need to establish colonies first and foremost with "the tillage of the soil, which is yet almost the sole occupation wherein innocence may be found." Lescarbot was a French lawyer who had lived for a short time in the small settlement of Port-Royal. He partially attributed the previous failure of French attempts to establish a colony on the southeastern coast of North America to the neglect of this agricultural imperative (Lescarbot [1907] 1968, 284).

3 In the previous century, Michel de Montaigne had written in his famous essay "On Cannibals" that the peoples of Brazil "are wild, just as we call wild the fruits that Nature has produced by herself and in her normal course; whereas really it is those that we have changed artificially and led astray from the common order that we should rather call wild" (1946, 205). As an essayist and social critic, Montaigne was one of the first to use an image of noble or innocent savagery derived from the New World – the *bon sauvage* – as a literary device in commentary on contemporary social and political life in Europe.

4 There is an interesting ambiguity in the *Relations* between this implicit gendering of all Aboriginal recipients of the seed as feminine, and the Jesuits' depictions – discussed in greater detail later in this chapter – of the outstanding masculine form and physical strength of Aboriginal men, as well as women. During the period I deal with in this analysis, the Jesuits did not rely on an idea that the French, and specifically French men, represented the ideal physical form of humanity. See Ann McClintock (1995, 55) on how, in other eras and contexts, colonial discourses gendered African men as feminine in descriptions of their bodies and habits. These discourses engaged the idea that the white European male was indeed more perfect in physical beauty as well as viability, and by depicting

colonized men in feminine terms made the latter doubly less than the white men who ruled them.

5 Many of the most signature instances of conversion in the Christian tradition were initiated orally, by voice and not by text. Paul's experience on the road to Damascus, for example, was one of being blinded by light and then hearing the voice of Christ, and Christ is repeatedly described in the New Testament as "orally proclaiming the good news of salvation to those around him, just as he eventually sends out his apostles to preach his message" (Rafael 1993, 40–1). Le Jeune reflected this history, as well as Paul's advice to the Romans, when he wrote that "*Fides ex auditu*, faith enters by the ear" (5:191).

6 For a recent treatment of theories of diffusion and homogeneous origins in the context of interpretations of the New World, see MacCormack 1995.

7 Before this, Marc Lescarbot had written: "I have another argument which may serve to prove that these peoples have been borne there in this manner, i.e. by shipwreck, and that they have sprung from a race of men who had been taught the law of God. For one day when M. de Poutrincourt was speaking through an interpreter with a Savage chief named Chkoudun, concerning our faith and religion, on being told of the Flood he replied that he had indeed long ago heard that in ancient times there had been wicked men who died one and all, and that better had come in their places. And this legend of the Flood prevails not only in the part of New France wherein we dwelt, but also among the tribes of Peru"([1907] 1968, 46). While Lescarbot advanced a variety of possibilities to account for the peopling of North America, including migration across the Bering Strait, he suggested that because of this "obscure knowledge of the Flood ... what hinders us from believing that Noah during his life of 350 years after the Flood did not himself see to it, and take pains to people, or rather to repeople, these lands?" (ibid., 47).

8 See Revelations 20:12–15: "And I saw the dead, great and small, standing before the throne, and books were opened. Also another book was opened, which is the book of life. And the dead were judged by what was written in the books, by what they had done. And the sea gave up the dead in it, Death and Hades gave up the dead in them, and all were judged by what they had done. Then Death and Hades were thrown into the lake of fire. This is the second death, the lake of fire; and if anyone's name was not found written in the book of life, he was thrown into the lake of fire."

9 Greenblatt (1991, 146) usefully draws our attention to the comment
of an English serving woman who, having been taken captive by
an unidentified Algonkian group, reported after her release that her
life had been hard, but no harder than her life as a serving woman
at home.

10 Several years later, Barthélemy Vimont attributed an entirely dissimi-
lar statement to an unidentified non-Christian at Tadoussac: "Father
Buteux was speaking one day in a cabin on the immortality of the
soul, adducing arguments of convenience, and even taking these
from some of their own principles, – as, for instance, what they said
formerly, that the souls of the deceased went to reside in a village
toward the setting Sun, where they hunt Beavers and Elk, carry on
war, and do the same things that they did in this life through the
agency of the senses. After this discourse, the savage, who had never
heard our Fathers speak on that subject, said: 'Why dost thou take
the trouble of proving that to us? One would be very foolish to
doubt it. We see very well that our soul is different from that of a
dog; the latter can perceive nothing that does not come under its
senses. But the soul of a man knows many things that are not perceived by the senses; and so it can act without the body, and without the senses. And if it can act without the body, it can exist
without the body. Therefore it is not material, and consequently it is
immortal'" (26:125–7).

11 Ignatius cautioned against excessive penances: "What appears most
suitable and most secure with regard to penance is that the pain
should be sensible in the flesh and not enter within the bones, so
that it give pain and not illness. For this it appears to be more suitable to scourge oneself with thin cords, which give pain exteriorly,
rather than in another way which would cause notable illness
within" (Fleming 1978, 56).

12 The Jesuits used this comparison in their attempts to communicate
their Christian message, incorporating images of torture reflective of
Aboriginal practice in their pictorial representations of hell as well as
in their teaching and catechisms. While the Jesuits' emphasis on hell
and punishment was not always successful, the skill with which they
incorporated torture into their teaching is reflected in their recognition of the differences they needed to stress in order for the imagery
to be effective. Because warriors were expected to endure pain
bravely and earned admiration for doing so, the priests took care to
emphasize that the fires of hell would be unendurable to even the

most courageous, both because these fires were more severe than those of this world and because they were never ending (Steckley 1992, 489–90). The Jesuits also stressed that, contrary to the ideals and expectations surrounding warfare and the conduct of warriors in the present life, in hell there would be no recognition of bravery and no honour for warriors – but rather contempt, mockery, and the shame that would come from being among those whose offences had caused them to be condemned by God (ibid., 492).

13 Fears of the real or imagined cannibalism of others were not limited to Europeans. When Martin Frobisher attempted the Northwest Passage in the 1570s, he and his men were afraid that the Inuit they encountered might want to eat them; the Inuit, however, were apparently as concerned that Frobisher and his men might themselves be cannibals (Greenblatt 1991, 111).

14 Guy Laflèche (1988; 1989) has argued that the deaths of the Jesuits who came to be known as the Canadian Martyrs were depicted according to a conventional formula and that the events represented in the *Relations* were manipulated in order to achieve the impression of martyrdom. With respect to the death of Isaac Jogues, Laflèche suggests that the Jesuit superior, Jérôme Lalemant, sent Jogues to the Iroquois during a temporary truce with the expectation that Jogues would be killed, and that he would then be able to construct a narrative account of Jogues's torture and death as a martyr to the faith (1989, 10).

15 Ann Stoler (1991, 1995) discusses fears of racial degeneracy in a variety of European colonial empires in Asia and Africa in the early twentieth century. In this context of late empire, it became European women's duty to protect racial continuity and racial purity by bearing children and by ensuring that their men would not turn to colonized women as sexual partners and thus suffer the moral and physical degeneration associated with life in the Tropics (ibid., 72–6). Stoler's work, here as elsewhere, (1995) treats whiteness as a constructed category. Racial membership and national belonging in the colonies could not be taken for granted on the basis of skin colour but was defined, as she notes, by "middle class morality, nationalist sentiments, bourgeois sensibilities, normalized sexuality," and a careful attention to racial and sexual hygiene in schools and the domestic sphere (1995, 105). In this way, whiteness, or Europeanness, was protected against the decay that was possible in a colonial context and was limited to a specific class, while subordinate races and

classes were viewed not just as degenerate in themselves but as potentially harmful influences on the racial and national purity of their masters and their masters' children.

CHAPTER FOUR

1 The Nipissing were an Algonkian-speaking people who lived to the northeast of the Huron, in the vicinity of Lake Nipissing. They traded directly with the French and their Huron neighbours, and frequently spent the winter in Huron country, trading furs and fish for Huron corn (21:239–41).

2 See also Foucault (1988, 73–85) for a discussion of the meaning of "the police" in the seventeenth and eighteenth centuries and its role in the rationality of state power.

3 During the epidemics that swept the Huron country, the Jesuits reported the suspicion held by some Huron that the disease was the work of Brûlé's uncle "in revenge for the death of his nephew, for which no satisfaction had been obtained" (14:17).

4 The debate on Jesuit laxity was complex and included theological issues of grace and free will that cannot be fully addressed here; however, it can be said that the standards that were advocated by the elite of the church throughout the seventeenth century had little to do with the reality of life for most people.

5 Here I use "competence" in the sense used by Bourdieu (1977) in his discussion of language and power and his critique of Chomskyan linguistics. In Chomskyan linguistics, "competence" refers to a speaker's ability to form grammatically correct sentences. Bourdieu argues that this does not sufficiently take into account the context and function of speech. For Bourdieu, the ability to form correct sentences is nothing without a mastery of the "conditions for adequate use" of these sentences (1977, 646). The "whole truth of the communicative relation is never fully present in the discourse, nor even in the communicative relation itself," but instead must be sought "outside discourse, in the social conditions of the production and reproduction of the producers and receivers and of their relationship" (1977, 650). Whereas the Chomskyan notion of "competence" takes the establishment of the conditions of communication for granted, or at least does not consider them important to the study of speech, Bourdieu argues that these conditions and their establishment cannot be separated from speech acts and are in fact

the primary issues for analysis. From this argument Bourdieu derives an expanded definition of "competence" as not only the ability to use language correctly but as "the right to speech" and the right to the language of authority (1977, 647).

6 The *donnés* were lay assistants who worked for the Jesuits without remuneration and under a number of binding conditions. These included the agreement to give up all personal possessions, to obey the superior of the mission, and to remain celibate. In return, the Jesuits provided the *donnés* with clothing, food, and lodging and cared for them in the event of sickness and in their old age (Trigger 1987, 575).

7 The Jesuits at the court of the Mogul emperor Akbar in the sixteenth century behaved toward the emperor with the respect and deference they would expect any monarch to receive. Their letters from the court report positively on the emperor's behaviour as a ruler and note that his subjects both loved and feared him (Correia-Afonso 1980, 22, 37). While they reported frequent conflicts with the religious authorities at the court, they did not fail to recognize Islam as a religion and a body of law.

8 Vimont alluded to this when he commented in general that "although they are void of humility, and have an entire freedom to do and say whatever they like in their cabins, nevertheless, in the matter of reproving one another, they proceed with a strange circumspection and prudence" (24:83).

9 Jesuit reductions in Paraguay were established in 1609 and were maintained until the Jesuits were expelled in 1767 (Trigger 1987, 577).

10 Le Jeune had not been in New France for very long before he commented on relations between men and women: "The women have great power here. A man may promise you something, and, if he does not keep his promise, he thinks he is sufficiently excused when he tells you that his wife did not wish to do it" (5:181). Le Jeune told one man who offered him this excuse "that he was the master, and that in France women do not rule their husbands" (5:181). In New France the Jesuit's attitude toward women and their assumptions about women's proper relationship to men were those of the androcentric, patriarchal society of which they were a part; they generally assumed women to be the physical, intellectual, and spiritual inferiors of men (cf. Briggs 1989, 250).

11 One woman who had been a legitimate wife in terms of local marriage became, in the Jesuits' terms, "that concubine, by whom he has

children" and was said to have "charmed" her husband again, "insomuch that, being cured, – for he was sick, – he fell back into her snares" (31:269). Women frequently appeared in the *Relations* as catalysts for men's sexual transgressions – as defined by the Jesuits – and bore the brunt of responsibility for those transgressions. In describing a Christian convert who had taken a "concubine" but had subsequently been convinced of the need to reform and repent, Lalemant wrote: "Even after all this, he may relapse. He fears this, and has begged me to manage so that he may not be where that wretched woman is who has been his rock of scandal" (25:281). Another baptized and monogamously married man was "enticed by a woman" (29:103) and consequently abandoned by the Jesuits. The man sought out a priest to confess and was reported to have said: "When that woman who has ruined me was endeavoring to gain me, I fled from her, at first; but little by little I took pleasure in her friendship. I thought no harm in that, until I realized that my heart desired to be wicked; I drove her away from me, but she went not far, – very soon, she appeared before my eyes. Finally I began to love; my heart trembled, reproaching me that I would forsake prayer. I was going to confess at once; but this demon, pursuing me, ruined me" (29:105).

CHAPTER FIVE

1 In an especially interesting literal play on the Jesuits' insistence that the Bible was the unmediated, directly transmitted Word of God, Le Jeune reported: "When I told them that we had a book which contained the words and teachings of God, they were very anxious to know how we could have gotten this book, – some of them believing that it had been let down from the Sky at the end of a rope, and that we had found it thus suspended in the air" (11:209).

2 Indeed, while the smallpox epidemics ultimately passed, Native critiques of writing were not without prescience of the larger ramifications of entering history. One man, upon being told that his people were dying as a result of the overconsumption of the brandy used in the fur trade, retorted: "It is not these drinks that take away our lives, but your writings; for since you have described our country, our rivers, our lands, and our woods, we are all dying, which did not happen until you came here" (9:207). The Jesuits denied these deleterious consequences of writing the New World into a history

that embraced the inhabitants with alien pathogens at the same time as it was supposed to proffer them the means of salvation, by explaining to this man that they "described the whole world" without similarly harmful effects (9:207).

3 A recent attribution of these diseases to the Europeans' abandonment of the "laws of nature" and more general alienation from the natural world (Sioui 1992, 3–7) is as embedded in the assumption of a universally applicable schema of laws, causes, and effects as the attributions of the Jesuits. While it may be meant to refute such statements as the priests inititialy made and to represent the real truth, it matches them in the assumption that the cultural and religious dictates of one people – including an understanding of the natural world and the appropriate human relationships with it – are not, in effect, creations but represent reality as a given, and that, as such, they can be universally binding as a yardstick with which to judge and understand the history, behaviour, and beliefs of other peoples.

4 Aboriginal people who reportedly resisted or abused Christianity were not the only victims of God's anger and punishment in the *Relations*. The Jesuits represented the untimely death of French Protestants in a similar manner (5:233; 6:105–7).

5 Lamberville's *Relation* is one of the very few to have survived in both the original and the edited version. These statements were among the material deleted in the final published work.

6 The Jesuits' use of a military metaphor was not limited to descriptions of their own activities. This imagery was equally pervasive in the catechisms prepared for use by converts or would-be converts to Christianity. In these, "the whole piece is set as a battle between opposing sides: God versus Devil, Jesuit versus shaman, converts versus pagans" (Axtell 1985, 110). The details of the imagery, however, were drawn from the Jesuits' knowledge of Aboriginal warfare. Axtell (ibid.) has argued that the Jesuits' skilful use of analogies referring to experiences that were readily familiar to many Huron greatly contributed to their success as missionaries.

7 The Jesuits frequently used the word "nation" to refer to indigenous groups. However, although the Jesuits, no less than French traders and administrators, recognized Native groups as individual entities with whom military and trading alliances could and should be made, they did not equate them with what they knew as the sovereign states of Europe (Jaenen 1984, 31). More specifically, the

word "nation" was not at this time synonymous with a self-governing polity, nor was it considered to be the natural basis for one; thus the Jesuits were able to use a term that is currently associated with rights to self-government to denote peoples they often characterized as lacking government. Historically, the modern political sense of "nation," in which it is conceived as coterminous with a state and associated with inalienable rights to both sovereignty and territory, was not relevant in Europe prior to the eighteenth century. The definition of nations on the basis of homogeneity of either ethnicity or language is an even more recent phenomenon and, in the case of language, was not possible before the era of mass literacy, print media, and standardized education (Hobsbawm 1990, 10, 52). Benedict Anderson's (1991, 44–3) well-known and influential discussion of nations as imagined political communities emphasizes the role of print capitalism in enabling this imagining to take place.

Although the Jesuits' entry into North America coincided with developments in the consolidation of centralized states in Europe, this consolidation still resulted in monarchical states in which kings ruled by divine right over a diverse and polyglot assortment of primarily illiterate subjects, rather than over a population of citizens who imagined themselves bound by a common destiny, much less a common language. It had also occurred at the expense of an earlier, medieval universalism, in which the various sub-units of Europe had seen themselves as part of a more inclusive Christian polity (Kohn 1944, 187). Indeed, before the eighteenth century the political arrangements of Europe, no less than Asia and Africa, had encompassed a variety of "nations" within larger polities.

CONCLUSION

1 These discourses demonstrate how resistance to colonialism may be effective through the appropriation and deployment of some of its forms of knowledge. Some authors draw attention to the ways in which such discourses, to the extent that they assert alternate but equally oppositional totalities of colonizers and colonized, perpetuate the representational techniques, orders of knowledge, and essentialist logic that inform the categories and oppositions they reject (e.g., Abu-Lughod 1993, 10). Other authors argue that it is wrong to dismiss these discourses as solely oppositional responses that merely mimic colonial categories; certainly, doing so implies that the

colonized can never escape the colonization of their imaginations (Chatterjee 1994, 5). Focusing on India, Partha Chatterjee (1994) argues that while the idea of the nation is indeed a product of Europe, and while nations are indeed "imagined communities," the anticolonial nationalism that emerged in India in the nineteenth century did not merely mimic a form of nationalism and national society available from existing European examples. This is because Indian anticolonial nationalism advocated a national society that would emulate the West in matters of "economy and statecraft, of science and technology," but not in matters of culture and spirituality. The latter, according to Chatterjee (1993, 6), emerged as the distinct realm of anticolonial nationalism's sovereignty before the anticolonial movement began its political battle. In this domain, Chatterjee argues, nationalism launched "its most powerful, creative, and historically significant project: to fashion a 'modern' national culture that is nevertheless not Western. If the nation is an imagined community, then this is where it is brought into being" (ibid., 6).

2 The priests also indicate that their knowledge of the real character of Aboriginal people is important in appreciating the significance of the transformation from the pagan to the Christian. When the Jesuits advised a young Christian Huron that it was improper for him to live in the longhouse of his future wife, he immediately agreed to leave. When Lalemant reported on this behaviour, he remarked: "This obedience, contrary to the Savages' customs among young people who are mutually in love, resembles a miracle in the minds of those who know the character of these tribes" (31:169). As as I have shown, this character has previously been described as disobedient and unrestrained. The use of "tribes" here is, it should be noted, the nineteenth-century English translation of *peuples* (31:168).

3 A similar generalizing logic informs another statement, written some years later, attributing the opposite characteristics: "Read the foregoing Relations, and you will find that the Savages are as susceptible to the Divine influence as are other and more civilized nations. The gift of prayer, the love of suffering, and charity toward one's neighbor, are found in some in an eminent degree ... From the sample the whole piece is known" (44:253).

References

Abu-Lughod, Lila. 1993. *Writing Women's Worlds: Bedouin Stories.* Berkeley, Los Angeles, and Oxford: University of California Press

Altherr, Thomas L. 1983. "'Flesh is the Paradise of a Man of Flesh': Cultural Conflict over Indian Hunting Beliefs and Rituals in New France as Recorded in *The Jesuit Relations.*" *Canadian Historical Review* 64:267–76

Anderson, Benedict. 1991. *Imagined Communities.* 2nd edn. London and New York: Verso

Anderson, Karen. 1991. *Chain Her by One Foot: The Subjugation of Native Women in Seventeenth-Century New France.* New York and London: Routledge

Aveling, J.C.H. 1981. *The Jesuits.* London: Blond and Briggs

Axtell, James. 1985. *The Invasion Within: The Contest of Cultures in Colonial North America.* New York and Oxford: Oxford University Press

– 1988. *After Columbus: Essays in the Ethnohistory of Colonial North America.* New York and Oxford: Oxford University Press

Bailey, Alfred G. 1969. *The Conflict of European and Eastern Algonkian Cultures, 1504–1700.* 2nd edn. Toronto: University of Toronto Press

Beaulieu, Alain. 1990. *Convertir les fils de Caïn: Jésuites et Amérindiens nomades en Nouvelle-France, 1632–1642.* Quebec: Nuit Blanche Editeur

Berkhofer, Robert F. 1979. *The White Man's Indian: Images of the American Indian from Columbus to the Present.* New York: Vintage Books

Bernheimer, Richard. 1970. *Wild Men in the Middle Ages: A Study in Art, Sentiment, and Demonology.* New York: Octagon Books

Berthiaume, Pierre. 1995. "Les Relations des jésuites: Nouvel avatar de la Légend dorrée." In *Figures de l'Indien,* ed. Gilles Therrien, 129–58. Montreal: Typo

Bhabha, Homi. 1994. *The Location of Culture*. London and New York: Routledge

Biggar, H.P. [1922–36] 1971. *The Works of Samuel de Champlain*. 6 vols. Toronto and Buffalo: University of Toronto Press

Bloch Maurice, and Jean H. Bloch. 1980. "Women and the Dialectics of Nature in Eighteenth-Century French Thought." In *Nature, Culture, and Gender*, ed. C. MacCormack and M. Strathern, 25–41. Cambridge: Cambridge University Press

Bourdieu, Pierre. 1977. "The Economics of Linguistic Exchanges." *Social Science Information* 16:645–68. Beverley Hills: Sage Publications

Bowker, John. 1970. *Problems of Suffering in the Religions of the World*. Cambridge: Cambridge University Press

Briggs, Robin. 1986. "Idées and Mentalités: The Case of the Catholic Reform Movement in France." *History of European Ideas* 7, no. 1: 9–19

– 1989. *Communities of Belief: Cultural and Social Tension in Early Modern France*. Oxford: Clarendon Press

Brockliss, L.W.B. 1987. *French Higher Education in the Seventeenth and Eighteenth Centuries: A Cultural History*. Oxford: Clarendon Press

Campeau, Lucien, SJ. 1987. *La mission des Jésuites chez les Hurons, 1634–1650*. Montreal: Editions Bellarmin; and Rome: Institutum Historicum SI

Chatterjee, Partha. 1993. *The Nation and Its Fragments*. Princeton: Princeton University Press

Church, William F. 1972. *Richelieu and Reason of State*. Princeton: Princeton University Press

– 1975. "France." In *National Consciousness, History, and Political Culture in Early Modern Europe*, ed. Orest Ranum, 43–66. Baltimore and London: Johns Hopkins University Press

Clark, Kenneth. 1952. *Landscape into Art*. London: John Murray

Clifford, James. 1986. "Introduction: Partial Truths." In *Writing Culture: The Poetics and Politics of Ethnography*, ed. James Clifford and George E. Marcus, 1–26. Berkeley: University of California Press

– 1988. *The Predicament of Culture: Twentieth-Century Ethnography, Literature, and Art*. Cambridge: Harvard University Press

Codignola, Luca. 1995. "The Holy See and the Conversion of the Indians in French and British North America, 1486–1760." In *America in European Consciousness, 1493–1750*, ed. Karen Ordahl Kupperman, 195–242. Chapel Hill: University of North Carolina Press

Cohn, Bernard S. 1985. "The Command of Language and the Language of Command." In *Subaltern Studies: Writings on South Asian History and Society.* Vol. 4, ed. R. Guha, 276–329. Oxford: Oxford University Press

Comaroff, Jean, and John Comaroff. 1991. *Of Revelation and Revolution: Christianity, Colonialism, and Consciousness in South Africa.* Vol. 1. Chicago: University of Chicago Press

– 1992. *Ethnography and the Historical Imagination.* Boulder: Westview Press

Comaroff, John. 1997. "Images of Empire, Contests of Conscience." In *Tensions of Empire: Colonial Cultures in a Bourgeois World,* ed. Frederick Cooper and Ann Laura Stoler, 163–97. Berkeley and Los Angeles: University of California Press

Cooper, Frederick, and Ann Laura Stoler. 1997. "Between Metropole and Colony: Rethinking a Research Agenda." In *Tensions of Empire: Colonial Cultures in a Bourgeois World,* ed. Frederick Cooper and Ann Laura Stoler, 1–56. Berkeley and Los Angeles: University of California Press

Correia-Afonso, John, ed. 1980. *Letters from the Mughal Court: The First Jesuit Mission to Akbar (1580–1583).* Anand: Gujarat Sahitya Prakash

Crapanzano, Vincent. 1986. "Hermes' Dilemma: The Masking of Subversion in Ethnographic Description." In *Writing Culture: The Poetics and Politics of Ethnography,* ed. James Clifford and George E. Marcus, 51–76. Berkeley: University of California Press

Dante [Dante Alighieri]. 1965. *The Divine Comedy.* Trans. Geoffrey L. Bickersteth. Revd edn, 1972. Oxford: Blackwell, for Shakespeare Head Press

Day, Gordon M., and Bruce G. Trigger. 1978. "Algonquin." In *The Handbook of North American Indians,* ed. William C. Sturtevant. Vol. 15, *The Northeast,* ed. Bruce Trigger, 792–7. Washington: Smithsonian Institution

de Guibert, Joseph, sj. 1964. *The Jesuits: Their Spiritual Doctrine and Practice.* Trans. William J. Young, sj. Chicago: Institute of Jesuit Sources in cooperation with Loyola University Press

Delâge, Denys. 1993. *Bitter Feast: Amerindians and Europeans in Northeastern North America, 1600–64.* Trans. Jane Brierley. Vancouver: University of British Columbia Press

Devens, Carol. 1992. *Countering Colonization: Native American Women and Great Lakes Missions, 1630–1900.* Berkeley and Los Angeles: University of California Press

Dickason, Olive P. 1984. *The Myth of the Savage and the Beginnings of French Colonialism in the Americas.* Edmonton: University of Alberta Press

Dirks, Nicholas B. 1992a. "Introduction: Colonialism and Culture." In *Colonialism and Culture*, ed. Nicholas B. Dirks, 1–25. Ann Arbor: University of Michigan Press

– 1992b. "From Little King to Landlord: Colonial Discourse and Colonial Rule." In *Colonialism and Culture*, ed. Nicholas B. Dirks, 175–208. Ann Arbor: University of Michigan Press

Duignan, Peter. 1958. "Early Jesuit Missionaries: A Suggestion for Further Study." *American Anthropologist* 60:725–32

Evennett, H.O. 1958. "The New Orders." In *The New Cambridge Modern History*. Vol. 2, *The Reformation, 1520–1559*, ed. G.R. Elton, 275–300. Cambridge: Cambridge University Press

Fabian, Johannes. 1983a. "Missions and the Colonization of African Languages: Developments in the Former Belgian Congo." *Canadian Journal of African Studies* 17:165–87

– 1983b. *Time and the Other: How Anthropology Makes Its Object*. New York: Columbia University Press

Ferland, Rémi. 1992. *Les Relations des Jésuites: Un art de la persuasion. Procédés de rhetorique et fonction conative dans les Relations du Père Paul Lejeune*. Quebec: Editions de la Huit

– 1993. "La citation biblique comme procédé conatif dans les *Relations* du père Lejeune." In *Rhétorique et conquête missionnaire: Le jésuite Paul Lejeune*, ed. Réal Ouellet, 25–39. Sillery: Editions du Septentrion

Fleming, David L., SJ. 1978. *The Spiritual Exercises of St Ignatius: A Literal Translation and a Contemporary Reading*. St Louis: Institute of Jesuit Sources

Foucault, Michel. 1979. *Discipline and Punish: The Birth of the Prison*. New York: Vintage Books

– 1980. *The History of Sexuality*. New York: Vintage Books

– 1988. *Politics, Philosophy, Culture: Interventions and Other Writings, 1977–1984*. Ed. Lawrence O. Kritzman. Routledge: New York and London

Francis, Daniel, and Toby Morantz. 1983. *Partners in Furs: A History of the Fur Trade in Eastern James Bay, 1600–1870*. Montreal and Kingston: McGill-Queen's University Press

Frye, Northrope. 1990. *The Great Code: The Bible and Literature*. London and New York: Penguin

Gagnon, François-Marc. 1984. *Ces hommes dits sauvages: L'histoire fascinante d'un préjugé qui remonte aux premiers decouvriers du Canada*. Montreal: Editions Libre Expression

Ganss, George E., trans. 1970. *The Constitutions of the Society of Jesus*. St Louis: Institute of Jesuit Sources

Gilroy, Paul. 1987. *"There Ain't No Black in the Union Jack": The Cultural Politics of Race and Nation.* Chicago: University of Chicago Press
– 1990. "One Nation under a Groove: The Cultural Politics of 'Race' and Racism in Britain." In *Anatomy of Racism*, ed. David Theo Goldberg, 263–82. Minneapolis: University of Minnesota Press
Grant, John Webster. 1984. *The Moon of Wintertime: Missionaries and the Indians of Canada in Encounter since 1534.* Toronto, Buffalo, and London: University of Toronto Press
Grassmann, Thomas. 1966. "Pierre-Antoine Pastedechouan." *Dictionary of Canadian Biography*, ed. George W. Brown et al., 1:533–4. Toronto: University of Toronto Press
Greenblatt, Stephen. 1991. *Marvelous Possessions: The Wonder of the New World.* Chicago: University of Chicago Press
Guha, Ranajit. 1989. "Dominance without Hegemony and Its Historiography." *Subaltern Studies* 6:210–309
Hall, Stuart. 1986. "Gramsci's Relevance for Race and Ethnicity." *Journal of Communication Inquiry* 10, no. 2: 5–27
Hammond, Dorothy, and Alta Jablow. 1970. *The Africa That Never Was: Four Centuries of British Writing about Africa.* New York: Twayne
Haraway, Donna. 1988. "Situated Knowledges: The Science Question in Feminism and the Privilege of Partial Perspective." *Feminist Studies* 14, no. 3: 575–99
Harrod, Howard L. 1984. "Missionary Life World and Native Response: Jesuits in New France." *Studies in Religion* 13, no. 2: 179–92
Hartog, François. 1988. *The Mirror of Herodotus: The Representation of the Other in the Writing of History.* Trans. Janet Lloyd. Berkeley, Los Angeles, and London: University of California Press
Healy, George R. 1958. "The French Jesuits and the Idea of the Noble Savage." *William and Mary Quarterly* 15, no. 2: 143–67
Heidenreich, Conrad E. 1971. *Huronia: A History and Geography of the Huron Indians, 1600–1650.* Toronto: McClelland and Stewart
– 1978. "Huron." In *The Handbook of North American Indians*, ed. William C. Sturtevant. Vol. 15, *The Northeast*, ed. Bruce Trigger, 368–88. Washington: Smithsonian Institution
Hobsbawm, E.J. 1990. *Nations and Nationalism since 1780: Programme, Myth, Reality.* Cambridge: Cambridge University Press
Hodgen, Margaret. 1964. *Early Anthropology in the Sixteenth and Seventeenth Centuries.* Philadelphia: University of Pennsylvania Press
Honour, Hugh. 1975. *The New Golden Land: European Images of America from the Discoveries of America to the Present Time.* New York: Pantheon Books, Random House

Jaenen, Cornelius J. 1974. "Amerindian Views of French Culture in the Seventeenth Century." *Canadian Historical Review* 55, no. 3: 261–91

– 1976. *The Role of the Church in New France.* Toronto: McGraw-Hill Ryerson

– 1984. *The French Relationship with the Native Peoples of New France and Acadia.* Paper prepared for Research Branch, Department of Indian and Northern Affairs, Canada

– 1985. "France's America and Amerindians: Image and Reality." *History of European Ideas* 6, no. 4: 405–20

Jetten, Marc. 1994. *Enclaves amérindiennes: Les "reductions" du Canada, 1637–1701.* Sillery: Editions du Septentrion

Kelley, Donald R. 1981. *The Beginning of Ideology: Consciousness and Society in the French Reformation.* Cambridge: Cambridge University Press

Keohane, Nannerl O. 1980. *Philosophy and the State in France: The Renaissance to the Enlightenment.* Princeton: Princeton University Press

Kidd, B.J. 1963. *The Counter-Reformation: 1550–1600.* London: Literature Association of the Church Union

Kohn, Hans. 1944. *The Idea of Nationalism: A Study in Its Origins and Background.* New York: Macmillan

Kondo, Dorrine. 1990. *Crafting Selves: Power, Gender, and Discourses of Identity in a Japanese Workplace.* Chicago and London: University of Chicago Press

Laflèche, Guy [with François-Marc Gagnon]. 1988. *Les saints martyrs canadiens.* Vol. 1, *Histoire du mythe.* Laval: Editions du Singulier

Laflèche, Guy. 1989. *Les saints martyrs canadiens.* Vol. 2, *Le martyre d'Isaac Jogues par Jérôme Lalemant.* Laval: Editions du Singulier

Lanctot, Gustave. 1963. *A History of Canada.* Vol. 1, *From Its Origins to the Royal Regime, 1663.* Trans. Josephine Hambleton. Toronto: Clarke, Irwin

Leacock, Eleanor. 1980. "Montagnais Women and the Jesuit Program for Colonization." In *Women and Colonization: Anthropological Perspectives,* ed. Mona Etienne and Eleanor Leacock, 25–42. New York: Praeger

– 1981. "Seventeenth-Century Montagnais Social Relations and Values." In *The Handbook of North American Indians,* ed. William C. Sturtevant. Vol. 6, *Subarctic,* ed. June Helm, 190–5. Washington: Smithsonian Institution

Le Bras, Yvon. 1994. *L'Amerindien dans les Relations du Père Paul Lejeune, 1632–1641.* Sainte-Foy: Editions de la Huit

Le Clercq, Chrestien. 1691. *Premier etablissement de la foy dans la Nouvelle France.* Paris

Leddy Phelan, John. 1970. *The Millennial Kingdom of the Franciscans in the New World*. Berkeley and Los Angeles: University of California Press

Lescarbot, Marc. [1907] 1968. *The History of New France*. 3 Vols. Trans. and ed. W.L. Grant, with introduction by H.P. Biggar. Toronto: Champlain Society. Reprint, New York: Greenwood Press

Lublinskaya, A.D. 1968. *French Absolutism: The Crucial Phase, 1620–1629*. Trans. Brian Pearce. Cambridge: Cambridge University Press

McClintock, Anne. 1995. *Imperial Leather: Race, Gender, and Sexuality in the Colonial Contest*. New York: Routledge

MacCormack, Sabine. 1995. "Limits of Understanding: Perceptions of Greco-Roman and Amerindian Paganism in Early Modern Europe." In *America in European Consciousness, 1493–1750*, ed. Karen Ordahl Kupperman, 79–129. Chapel Hill: University of North Carolina Press

Maland, David. 1970. *Culture and Society in Seventeenth-Century France*. New York: Charles Scribner's Sons

Mandrou, Robert. 1976. *Introduction to Modern France, 1500–1640: An Essay in Historical Psychology*. Trans. R.E. Hallmark. New York: Holmes and Meier

Mani, Lata. 1992. "Critical Theory, Colonial Texts: Reading Eyewitness Accounts of Widow Burning." In *Cultural Studies*, ed. Lawrence Grossberg, Cary Nelson, and Paula Treichler, 392–408. New York and London: Routledge

Martin, A. Lynn. 1973. *Henry III and the Jesuit Politicians*. Geneva: Librairie Droz

– 1988. *The Jesuit Mind: The Mentality of an Elite in Early Modern France*. Ithaca and London: Cornell University Press

Mignolo, Walter D. 1992. "On the Colonization of Amerindian Languages and Memories: Renaissance Theories of Writing and the Discontinuity of the Classical Tradition." *Comparative Studies in Society and History* 34, no. 4: 301–30

Montaigne, Michel de. 1946. *The Essays of Montaigne*. Trans. E.J. Trechman. New York and London: Oxford University Press

Morantz, Toby. 1982. "Northern Algonquian Concepts of Status and Leadership Reviewed: A Case Study of the Eighteenth-Century Trading Captain System." *Canadian Review of Sociology and Anthropology* 19, no. 4: 482–501

Morrison, Kenneth M. 1985. "Discourse and the Accommodation of Values: Toward a Revision of Mission History." *Journal of the American Academy of Religion* 53, no. 3: 365–82

– 1986. "Montagnais Missionization in Early New France: The Syncretic Imperative." *American Indian Culture and Research Journal* 10, no. 3: 1–23

– 1990. "Baptism and Alliance: The Symbolic Mediations of Religious Syncretism." *Ethnohistory* 37, no. 4: 416–37

Olin, John C. 1969. *The Catholic Reformation: Savonarola to Ignatius Loyola*. New York: Harper and Row

O'Malley, John W. 1993. *The First Jesuits*. Cambridge, Mass.: Harvard University Press

Ong, Walter J., SJ. 1967. *The Presence of the Word: Some Prolegema for Cultural and Religious History*. New Haven and London: Yale University Press

Ouellet, Réal. 1987. "Entreprise missionnaire et ethnographie dans les premières *Relations* de Le Jeune." In *Les jésuites parmi les hommes aux XVI et XVII siècles*. Clermont-Ferrand, France: Association des Publications de la Faculté des Lettres et Sciences Humaines de Clermont-Ferrand

– 1993. "Premières images du sauvage dans les écrits de Cartier, Champlain, et Lejeune." In *"L'Indien," Instance discursive: Actes du Colloque de Montreal, 1991,* ed. Antonio Gomez-Moriana and Danièle Trottier, 53–79. Quebec: Éditions Balzac

Ouellet, Réal, and Alain Beaulieu. 1993. "Avant-propos." In *Rhétorique et conquêt missionnaire: Le jésuite Paul Lejeune*, ed. Réal Ouellet, 9–24. Sillery: Editions du Septentrion

Parkman, Francis. [1867] 1927. *The Jesuits in North America in the Seventeenth Century*. Boston: Little, Brown

Parry, Benita. 1987. "Problems in Current Theories of Colonial Discourse." *Oxford Literary Review* 9, nos. 1–2: 27–58

Partridge, Eric. 1966. *Origins: A Short Etymological Dictionary of Modern English*. New York: Macmillan

Pioffet, Marie-Christine. 1993. "L'arc et l'épée: Les images de la guerre chez le jésuite Paul Lejeune." In *Rhétorique et conquête missionnaire: Le jésuite Paul Lejeune*, ed. Réal Ouellet, 41–52. Sillery: Editions du Septentrion

Pouliot, Léon. 1966. "Paul Le Jeune." *Dictionary of Canadian Biography*, ed. George W. Brown et al., 1:457–8. Toronto: University of Toronto Press

Prakash, Gyan. 1992. "Writing Post-Orientalist Histories of the Third World: Indian Historiography Is Good to Think." In *Colonialism and Culture*, ed. Nicholas B. Dirks, 353–88. Ann Arbor: University of Michigan Press

Pratt, Mary Louise. 1986. "Scratches on the Face of the Country; Or, What Mr. Barrow Saw in the Land of the Bushmen." In *"Race," Writing, and Difference*, ed. Henry Louis Gates, 138–62. Chicago: University of Chicago Press

Rafael, Vincente. 1993. *Contracting Colonialism: Translation and Christian Conversion in Tagalog Society under Early Spanish Rule*. Durham: Duke University Press

Ray, Arthur J. 1974. *Indians in the Fur Trade: Their Role as Trappers, Hunters, and Middlemen in the Lands Southwest of Hudson Bay*. Toronto: University of Toronto Press

Rogers, Edward S., and Eleanor Leacock. 1981. "Montagnais-Naskapi." In *The Handbook of North American Indians*, ed. William C. Sturtevant. Vol. 6, *Subarctic*, ed. June Helm, 169–89. Washington: Smithsonian Institution

Ronda, James P. 1979. "The Sillery Experiment: A Jesuit-Indian Village in New France, 1637–1663." *American Indian Culture and Research Journal* 3, no. 1: 1–18

Rosaldo, Renato. 1989. *Culture and Truth: The Remaking of Social Analysis*. Boston: Beacon Press

Rubiés, Joan-Pau. 1993. "New Worlds and Renaissance Ethnology." *History and Anthropology* 6, nos. 2–3: 157–97

Rushdie, Salman. 1991. *Imaginary Homelands*. London and New York: Penguin Books

Russell, Bertrand. 1946. *History of Western Philosophy and Its Connection with Political and Social Circumstances from the Earliest Times to the Present Day*. London: Allen and Unwin

Sagard, Gabriel. 1866. *Histoire du Canada*. Paris: Librairie Tross

– [1939] 1968. *The Long Journey to the Country of the Hurons*. Trans. H.H. Langton, ed. George M. Wrong. Toronto: Champlain Society

Said, Edward W. 1978. *Orientalism*. New York: Vintage Books, Random House

– 1993. *Culture and Imperialism*. New York: Knopf

Shennan, J.H. 1969. *Government and Society in France: 1461–1661*. London: Allen and Unwin

Sioui, Georges, E. 1992. *For an Amerindian Autohistory: An Essay on the Foundations of a Social Ethic*. Trans. Sheila Fischman. Montreal and Kingston: McGill-Queens University Press

– 1994. *Les Wendats: Une civilisation méconnue*. Sainte-Foy: Presses de l'Université Laval

Speck, Frank G. 1935. *Naskapi: The Savage Hunters of the Labrador Peninsula*. Norman: University of Oklahoma Press

Stallybrass, Peter, and Allon White. 1986. *The Politics and Poetics of Transgression*. London: Methuen

Steckley, John. 1992. "The Warrior and the Lineage: Jesuit Use of Iroquoian Images to Communicate Christianity." *Ethnohistory* 39, no. 4: 478–509

Stoler, Laura Ann. 1991. "Carnal Knowledge and Imperial Power: Gender, Race, and Morality in Colonial Asia." In *Gender at the Crossroads of Knowledge: Anthropology in the Postmodern Era*, ed. Micaela di Leonardo, 51–101. Berkeley: University of California Press

– 1995. *Race and the Education of Desire: Foucault's History of Sexuality and the Colonial Order of Things*. Durham: Duke University Press

Symcox, Geoffrey. 1972. "The Wild Man's Return: The Enclosed Vision of Rousseau's *Discourses*." In *The Wild Man Within: An Image in Western Thought from the Renaissance to Romanticism*, ed. Edward Dudley and Maximillian E. Novak, 223–47. Pittsburgh: University of Pittsburgh Press

Taylor, Mark C. 1984. *Erring: A Postmodern A/theology*. Chicago: University of Chicago Press

Tetlow, Elisabeth Meier, ed. and trans. 1987. *The Spiritual Exercises of St. Ignatius Loyola*. Lanham, Md: University Press of America

Thwaites, R.G. 1896–1901. *The Jesuit Relations and Allied Documents: Travels and Explorations of the Jesuit Missionaries in New France, 1610–1791*. Cleveland: Burrows Brothers

Tooker, Elisabeth. [1964] 1991. *An Ethnography of the Huron Indians, 1615–1649*. Syracuse: Syracuse University Press

– 1994. Review of *For an Amerindian Autohistory: An Essay on the Foundations of a Social Ethic* by Georges Sioui. *Anthropos* 89:309–10

Trigger, Bruce. 1966. "Amantacha." *Dictionary of Canadian Biography*, ed. George W. Brown et al., 1:58–9. Toronto: University of Toronto Press

– 1971. "Champlain Judged by His Indian Policy: A Different View of Early Canadian History." *Anthropologica* 13, nos. 1 & 2: 85–114

– 1982. "Ethnohistory: Problems and Prospects." *Ethnohistory* 29, no. 1: 1–19

– 1985. *Natives and Newcomers: Canada's "Heroic Age" Reconsidered*. Montreal and Kingston: McGill-Queens University Press

– 1987. *The Children of Aataentsic: A History of the Huron People to 1660*. 2 vols. Montreal and Kingston: McGill-Queen's University Press

Trudel, Marcel. 1973. *The Beginnings of New France: 1524–1663*. Toronto: McClelland and Stewart

Vaughan, Alden T. 1982. "From White Man to Redskin: Changing Anglo-American Perceptions of the American Indian." *American Historical Review* 87, no. 4: 917–53

Wagner, Roy. 1981. *The Invention of Culture*. Chicago: University of Chicago Press

Wallerstein, Immanuel. 1974. *The Modern World-System*. Vol. 1, *Capitalist Agriculture and the Origins of the European World-Economy in the Sixteenth Century*. New York: Academic Press

White, Hayden. 1972. "The Forms of Wildness: Archaeology of an Idea." In *The Wild Man Within: An Image in Western Thought from the Renaissance to Romanticism*, ed. Edward Dudley and Maximillian Novak, 3–38. Pittsburgh: University of Pittsburgh Press

– 1976. "The Noble Savage Theme as Fetish." In *First Images of America: The Impact of the New World on the Old*. Vol. 1, ed. Fredi Chiappelli, 121–35. Berkeley, Los Angeles, and London: University of California Press

Williams, Patrick, and Laura Chrisman. 1994. "Introduction." In *Colonial Discourse and Post-Colonial Theory: A Reader*, ed. Patrick Williams and Laura Chrisman, 1–20. New York and London: Harvester Wheatsheaf

Williams, Raymond. 1988. *Keywords: A Vocabulary of Culture and Society*. London: Fontana Press

Wolf, Eric. 1982. *Europe and the People without History*. Berkeley, Los Angeles, and London: University of California Press

Wroth, Lawrence C. 1936. "The Jesuit Relations from New France." Bibliographic Society of America. *Papers* 30:110–49

Young, Robert C. 1995. *Colonial Desire: Hybridity in Theory, Culture, and Race*. London and New York: Routledge

Index

absolutism, 29, 146n5
agriculture: importance of, 19, 42–5, 147n2; and Jesuits' preference for the Huron, 52; as metaphor for mission, 19, 46–8; opposed to wandering, 52
Algonkian: defined, 146n8
Algonkin: defined, 146n8; as middlemen in fur trade, 36
Altherr, Thomas, 59
Amantacha, Louis, 82–3
Anderson, Karen, 12, 98
Argall, Samuel, 21
Aveling, J.C.H, 123
Axtell, James, 7, 109, 123

Bailey, Alfred G., 31, 33, 95
baptism: Huron interpret as a healing rite, 111; interpreted as witchcraft, 111
Beaulieu, Alain, 12, 95
Berkhofer, Robert F., 7, 46
Bernheimer, Richard, 49, 56, 69
Bhabba, Homi, 10, 111, 135
Biard, Pierre, 21, 23
Biencourt de Poutrincourt, Jean de, 21

Biggar, H.P., 13, 36, 63, 71, 74, 76–80
Bloch, Jean H., 44
Bloch, Maurice, 44
Bourdieu, Pierre, 89
Bowker, John, 117
Brébeuf, Jean de, 7, 27, 31, 37, 43, 52, 56–7, 60–1, 63, 74, 83, 86–9, 106–9, 115–16; begins Huron mission, 38–9; death of, 40; as a martyr, 65–7; as orator, 88; use of physical mortifications, 59; and rainmaking, 106–7
Bressani, François, 65, 121
bridles, 30, 72
Briggs, Robin, 23–4, 57, 85
Brockliss, L.W.B., 24, 29
Brulé, Etienne, 82–3, 132

Caën, Emery de, 77; trading company, 27, 43
Campeau, Lucien, 6
cannibalism, 62–4; and savagery, 64
Carigonan, 33–4, 54, 58, 146n9
Cartier, Jacques, 31, 144–5n14
Champlain, Samuel de, 5, 21, 30; on Aboriginal

government and law, 71, 74; allies the French with the Montagnais, 32; attempts to impose French justice, 80–4; as colony builder, 26, 77; and exchange of people, 13; and French-Huron trading alliance, 36, 39, 89; on justice, 79; refuses reparation payments, 77–8; on torture, 63
Chaumonot, Pierre-Joseph-Marie, 93
Cherououny, 75–8
Chrisman, Laura, 10
Christian Island, 39–40
Church, William F., 23, 29, 73, 75
civilization, 10, 63
Clark, Kenneth, 53
Clifford, James, 18, 96
Codignola, Luca, 40
Cohn, Bernard S., 9, 86
Colbert, Jean-Baptiste, 28
colonial discourse: and the creation of difference, 131–4
colonial discourse studies, 8–9; limits of, 12; purpose of, 9–10, 14, 135–6
colonialism: differences between, 16–17, 132,

138–9; and knowledge,
  9–10, 18; in New
  France, 14
colonization on the St
  Lawrence, 40
Comaroff, Jean, 14, 18,
  47, 68, 127
Comaroff, John, 11, 14,
  18, 47, 68, 127
Compagnie du Saint-
  Sacrament, 27
Company of One Hun-
  dred Associates, 27, 30,
  95
conquest: Jesuits' mission
  as, 123–5, 128–9
conversion: authenticity
  of, 6–7; Jesuit descriptions of, 4, 6; nature of
  Aboriginal understand-
  ings of, 101, 127; and
  necessity of obedience,
  19, 91–3, 96; and sub-
  mission, 91–3, 95, 98,
  125–6
Cooper, Frederick, 132,
  135
corporal punishment of
  children: Aboriginal
  views on, 70–1, 94;
  first use of among
  Huron, 94
Counter-Reformation,
  22–3
culture, 4, 18, 101, 142n4
customs: Jesuits' descriptions of, 5, 9, 133–4; as
  unchanging, 48, 134

Daniel, Antoine, 31, 83,
  110; begins Huron mis-
  sion, 38–9; death of,
  40; as a martyr, 65
Dante, 52
Davost, Ambroise, 31, 83;
  begins Huron mission,
  38–9
Day, Gordon M., 36
degeneration, 19, 54, 56,
  69
Dequen, Father, 116
Devens, Carol, 98

Dickason, Olive, 45–6
Dirks, Nicholas, 8, 12,
  14, 131
disease: effects of, 14;
  epidemics among the
  Huron, 106; Huron
  believe to be caused by
  witchcraft, 106; Jesuits
  view as punishment, 20,
  105, 113–15, 119–21;
  as a trial or test of
  faith, 116–17. See also
  witchcraft
donnés, 89, 152n6
Douart, Jacques, 89–90,
  99
dreams: importance
  among the Huron, 110
Druillettes, Gabriel, 44
Duignan, Peter, 85
Du Thet, Gilbert, 21

Enlightenment, 17, 49,
  136–8
Erie, 40
Europeans: Aboriginal
  impressions of, 16, 56,
  119. See also history
Evennett, H.O., 22
evolution, 49, 68, 136
eyewitnessing: and an
  author's credibility, 9,
  133, 144n9

Fabian, Johannes, 48–9
Fleming, David L., 59,
  124
flesh, opposed to mind,
  47–8
flood, 54–5, 148n7
force: in definition of
  colonialism, 123; use of
  in missions, 121–2
forest: and absence of history, 44; effects of living
  in, 49–50; importance of
  clearing, 44–5; as a site
  of purity, 50; as a threatening place, 44, 49; as a
  wilderness, 44–5
Foucault, Michel, 60, 63,
  73, 77

Francis, Daniel, 32
Frye, Northrop, 51, 53

Garnier, Charles, 59
Gilroy, Paul, 68
Grant, John Webster, 124,
  127
Grassmann, Thomas, 33
Greenblatt, Stephen, 17,
  126
Guha, Ranajit, 14

Hall, Stuart, 68
Hammond, Dorothy, 64
Haraway, Donna, 96
Harrod, Howard L., 66
Healy, George R., 8
hegemony, 14–15
Heidenreich, Conrad, 5,
  13, 33, 36, 40, 87
hell: Huron interpreta-
  tions of, 112
Herodotus, 144n9
history: assumed absence
  among New World peo-
  ples, 15, 46, 48–9, 55;
  Europeans as makers
  of, 15, 49
Hodgen, Margaret, 53–4,
  67
Honour, Hugh, 8, 85
Huguenots, 28
hunting: Jesuits' attempt
  to replace with agriculture, 50, 95; Jesuit
  opinions of, 51, 59;
  and life in the forest,
  49; and wildness, 51
Huron: economy, 35; first
  contact with the
  French, 32–3; as focus
  of Jesuits' mission, 35,
  39; influence of women
  among, 37; law, 86;
  location of, 35; political organization and
  governance, 36–7, 86;
  religion, 37–8; sha-
  mans, 38; trade with
  French, 35–6, 39; war-
  fare with Iroquois, 39–
  40, 62

Huron confederacy, 11, 36–7; destruction of, 39–40, 118

Ihonatiria, 40, 107, 115
Ile d'Orléans: Huron retreat to, 40
imperialism, political: and Christian mission, 123, 126–7, 129
Innu, 146n6
Iroquois: as cannibals, 64–5; confederacy, 39, 146n7; as enemies, 62, 65; Jesuit missions among, 40, 121; warfare against Huron, 39–40, 62; as wolves, 62, 64–5

Jablow, Alta, 64
Jaenen, Cornelius, 15, 44, 56
Jansenists, 24, 29
Jesuits: and accommodation, 23, 84–5, 90–1, 131; arrive at Quebec, 27; and Counter-Reformation, 22; disapprove of traders' behaviour, 17, 132; displace Recollets, 30–1; feared as witches, 20, 90, 106–8, 110–12, 115, 122; forced to leave Quebec, 30; founding of the order, 22; importance of missionary work to, 22, 145n2; learn Native languages, 88–9, 101–2; and martyrdom, 65–6; missions in Europe, 22–3, 85; mission policy, 23–4, 84–5, 131; and political influence, 145n4; purpose of the order, 22, 145n2, 145n3; seek knowledge about Aboriginal customs, 85–6, 88–9, 133–4; as soldiers of God, 123–4;

use of physical mortifications, 59–60, 149n11
Jesuit Relations, 4; cessation of publication, 141n2; as colonial texts, 11, 15; descriptions of Aboriginal customs and manners, 4–5, 9, 133–4; as official publications, 18; as sources, 4–8, 11, 137
Jetten, Marc, 94–5
Jogues, Isaac: as a martyr, 65, 121, 150n14

Kelley, David, 66, 72–3
Keohane, Nannerl O., 29, 72
Kichesipirini Algonkin, 36, 83
Kidd, B.J., 22
Kondo, Dorrine, 103

La Flèche, Jesuit college of, 27, 31
Lalemant, Charles, 27
Lalemant, Gabriel: death of, 40; as a martyr, 65–7
Lalemant, Jérôme, 24, 38, 49–50, 59, 75, 85–7, 89, 99–102, 110, 113–16, 119–22, 125–6, 139; on difficulty of Jesuits' mission, 91–2, 129–30; on Jogue's martyrdom, 65
Lamberville, Jean de, 121
languages, Aboriginal: Jesuits' motives in learning, 101–2; Jesuits pursue competence in, 88–9, 151–2n5
La Rochelle, 28, 30
Lauson, Jean de, 30
law: French legal system of, 73–4; Huron, 86–8; and power of the monarch in ancien regime, 73; and punishment, 72–3
Leacock, Eleanor, 34–5, 98

Le Bras, Yvon, 63
Le Clerq, Chrestien, 92
Leddy Phelan, John, 49
Le Jeune, 3–4, 6, 8–9, 12–13, 31, 46–9, 53–5, 57–63, 66, 70–2, 74–5, 79, 82–4, 88, 100–3, 105, 108–9, 113–14, 117, 119, 121–4, 128, 133–5; on agriculture, 42–3; argues with Carigonan, 34, 58; on hunting, 51; starts Sillery, 94; and use of punishment at Sillery, 95–7; winters with Montagnais, 33–5, 5
Le Mercier, François-Joseph, 102, 112–13, 115
Le Moyne, Simon, 110
Lescarbot, Marc, 147n2
Loyola, Ignatius: and founding of Jesuits, 22–4; on physical penance, 149n11; and use of force in missions, 121; and use of military imagery, 123
Lublinskaya, A.D., 28

Maland, David, 27
Mani, Lata, 14
Martin, A. Lynn, 22, 23
martyrdom: critique of Jesuits as martyrs, 150n14; importance of to Jesuits, 65–6; and death of Jesuits, 65
Massé, Enemond, 21, 23, 27, 31
metaphor: use of by Aboriginal speakers, 88
Mignolo, Walter, 55, 108–9
military metaphors: Jesuits' use of, 13, 123–5, 154n6
Mohawk, 39, 146n7
monogenesis: Jesuit theories of and Aboriginal responses, 53

Montagnais: economy, 33, 49; as enemies of Iroquois, 32; French ally themselves with, 32; location, 31; offer reparation payments to French, 76; ritual practices, 33–4; shamans among, 34; social organization, 35; trade with Europeans, 31–2
Montaigne, Michel de, 147n3
Montmagny, Governor Charles Huault de, 98, 122
Morantz, Toby, 32, 74
Morrison, Kenneth, 5–6

nation: idea of, 154–5n7
nationalism: anticolonial, 155–6n1
Neutral, 40
Nipissing, 36, 70, 132, 151n1
Nobili, Roberto de, 85
noble savage: and critique of European society, 143n8, 147n3; contemporary idea of, 138; Relations as sources of, 7–8, 138, 143nn7 & 8
Noüe, Anne de, 31

Olin, John C., 22
O'Malley, John W., 22–4, 47, 124, 126
Ong, Walter, 47
oral practice: in mission, 47, 109, 148n5
oratory: importance of, 37, 88
Ossossané, 93, 111, 115
Ottawa River: as trade route, 82
Ouellet, Réal, 12, 66, 101

Parkman, Francis, 137
Parry, Benita, 16
Partridge, Eric, 52

passions: theories of the, 57
Pastedechouan, Pierre, 33, 146n9
Pioffet, Marie-Christine, 12
police, 70, 72, 151n2
polygamy: Jesuits' attempt to replace with monogamy, 98
Port-Royal, 21
Pouliot, Léon, 27, 31
Prakash, Gyan, 9, 16, 49
Pratt, Mary Louise, 48
primitive, 17; as a temporal condition, 49
progress, 17; and evolution, 68; idea of, 68, 136, 139
Protestants: presence of in New France, 25–6, 43, 154n4
public penance: use of by Aboriginal converts, 99
punishment: Aboriginal responses to threat of eternal punishment, 103; and law, 72–3; leads to conversion, 96, 119; and political authority, 72–4; use of at Sillery, 94, 96–9

Quentin, Jacques, 21

race and culture, 142n4; idea of, 68–9; and descriptions of Aboriginal people, 68; and nationality, 137
racial degeneracy: fears of, 150–1n15
Rafael, Vincente, 95, 103
Ragueneau, Paul, 61, 67, 89, 90, 118
Ray, Arthur, 32
Recollets, 26–7; forced to leave Quebec, 30; mission policy, 130–1; opinion of Aboriginal government and law, 71, 76, 88; opinion of

Aboriginal people, 26; replaced by Jesuits, 30
reductions, 94, 152n9
relativism: of Aboriginal people, 53, 101, 106, 127; of Jesuits, 86, 127, 130–1, 139
reparation payments, 70–1; among the Huron, 86–7; Jesuits accept from Huron, 84, 90–1; Jesuits' opinion of, 86, 88–9, 92; Montagnais offer to the French, 76; Recollets' opinion of, 76, 88
resistance, 15–16, 66–7, 111, 114–15
Richelieu, Cardinal, 27–8, 30, 73; and absolutism, 29; and state building, 28
Rogers, Edward S., 34
Ronda, James P., 95, 97
Rosaldo, Renato, 18
Rubiés, Joan-Pau, 44
Russell, Bertrand, 22

Sagard, Gabriel, 5, 37, 60, 76, 78
Said, Edward W., 9–10
Sainte-Marie, 39–40
sauvage: definition of, 45–6
savagery: and biology, 67–9; and bodily strength, 55–6; as a category, 9, 132; characteristics of, 19, 42, 46, 133–4; as culturally constructed, 135; and culture, 142n4; as fixed and knowable, 134–5; and the flesh, 57–9; and absence of government, 71; and absence of history, 48; and independence, 74–5, 92; and lawlessness, 75, 82–3; and torture, 63; relationship with the wilderness, 45–6

Seneca, 39, 82, 146n7
settlement of Aboriginal people: importance of to Jesuits, 35, 52, 94–5
sexual relations among Huron, 60; missionary views of, 60–1
Seysell, Claude de: and bridles, 72
shame as a legal sanction, 87
Shennan, J.H., 73
Sillery, 3, 6, 8, 94–6, 100; use of punishment at, 94, 96–9
Sillery, Noël Brulart de, 94
Sioui, Georges, 37, 110, 137
Society of Jesus. See Jesuits
sorcery. See witchcraft
Speck, Frank, 33
Spiritual Exercises, 59, 123–4
Stallybrass, Peter, 57
starvation: Huron suffer from, 40, 118
Steckley, John, 7
Stoler, Ann, 69, 132, 135
suffering: necessity of, 105, 117
Symcox, Geoffrey, 8

Taylor, Mark C., 53
Tetlow, Elisabeth Meier, 59
Thwaites, Rueben Gold, 3–4
time, 48–9
Tooker, Elisabeth, 5, 36, 40
torture: Aboriginal use of, 62–3, 74; in Europe, 63; Hurons'

use of Catholic ritual in, 67; of Jesuits, 65–6; Jesuits use images of in their mission, 149–50n12; and political authority, 73; and savagery, 63
trade: and colonization, 25–6, 43–4; and exchange of people between allies, 13–14; French-Huron trading alliance, 39, 82, 89–90, 123; Jesuits' objectives differ from those of traders, 17; and military alliances, 32; precedes missions in St Lawrence area, 25
translation, 47, 143n6; and accuracy of Aboriginal speeches in the Relations, 6–7; and difficulty of translating Christian concepts, 7, 93, 101–4, 136
Trigger, Bruce, 5, 7, 13, 26–7, 31–2, 36–7, 39–40, 67, 74, 77, 80, 82, 86–7, 89, 91, 93, 106–7, 123, 131–2, 137

Vaughan, Alden, 68
Ventadour, Duc de, 27
Vimont, Barthélemy, 31, 50, 64, 66, 74, 93, 99, 118, 122

Wallerstein, Immanuel, 28–9
wandering, 52–3; and theories of migration, 54. See also settlement
war as punishment, 116, 121

warfare: effects of, 14, 118; guerrilla, 62
Wendat, 146n6
Weskarini Algonkin, 81
White, Allon, 57
White, Hayden, 44–5, 51, 69
wilderness: in North America, 19; qualities of, 45. See also, savagery
Wild Man, 19, 45; biblical roots of Wild Man myth, 51; and degeneration, 56, 69
Williams, Patrick, 10
witchcraft: characteristics of among Huron, 106–7; Jesuits suspected of, 15, 20, 90, 106–8, 110–12, 115, 122; punishment for, among Huron, 87
Wolf, Eric, 18
women: Jesuits' effect on status of, 12; Jesuits' opinions of, 98, 143n7, 152n10, 152–3n11; and submission, 98
Word: ideology of the, 47; power of the, 46–7, 102, 113–14, 125; and writing, 109–10
writing: authority of, 55, 108–9; and civilization, 55, 109; and history, 55; impresses Aboriginal people, 109; superiority of over oral tradition, 55, 108–9; as witchcraft, 108–10, 153n2

Young, Robert C., 9, 12, 44, 123